LOOKING THROUGH THE EYES OF A DISCIPLEMAKER

VOLUME TWO

Herb Hodges

LOOKING THROUGH THE EYES OF A DISCIPLE-MAKER

VOLUME TWO

©2010 Herb Hodges

ALL RIGHTS RESERVED

No part of this publication may be reproduced, stored in a retrieval system, or transmitted in any form without prior written permission.

Spiritual Life Ministries
2916 Old Elm Lane
Germantown, TN 38138
Herb Hodges -- Executive Director
E-mail – herbslm@mindspring.com

Table of Contents

Chapter 13
Characteristics of a Christian – 9

Chapter 14
The Disciple-Maker's Final Balance Sheet - 19

Chapter 15
The Transforming Friendship - 37

Chapter 16
The Divine Drama of Salvation - 55

Chapter 17
Wanted: Men who will Follow the Model - 69

Chapter 18
What about Lost Church Members? - 87

Chapter 19
A Colony of Heaven on Earth - 99

Chapter 20
A Disciple's Checkpoint - 119

Chapter 21
The Infallible Sign of the Presence of God - 139

Chapter 22

Christianity 101 - 149

Chapter 23

Something to Think About - 165

Chapter 24

The Secret of Serenity – 179

Chapter 25

Behind the Seens - 197

Chapter 26

God's Promise of Provision - 209

Chapter 27

Saints under Satan's Nose - 221

Introduction

Have you ever accidentally come across a box of old letters in an attic? Multiplied millions of such letters must be stored in attics and closets around the world. I have in my library several volumes of letters written by renowned people. Some of them comprise very insightful and valuable reading to a Christian. However, none of them can match the importance of an old letter written by an old missionary nearly 2000 years ago, and kept in the old library of letters and books which we call the Bible. The old letter is a brief epistle written by the aging apostle Paul to a growing fellowship of Christian believers in the Roman colony of Philippi in what we now recognize as southern Europe. The letter to the Philippians is perhaps the greatest pastoral document ever written. Because it was written by a skilled disciple-maker, its purpose was to make and mature Christian disciples.

Our Bible has been divided into chapters and verses for our convenience in reading and studying it. However, we must remember that the epistle to the Philippians was a personal letter, and was not divided into such units. If we can imagine it handwritten and occupying the page like a letter, we may better get the feel of its message. Let me encourage you to read the above passage in at least two other good translations of the New Testament before you go further in this study. One of the most serious mistakes we make in Bible study is to suppose that we know what is in a book, or chapter, or paragraph, or sentence of Scripture just because we have previously read it. The experience of multitudes of Bible students through the centuries is entirely to the contrary.

We say that we "know" a man when we first meet him. In reality, however, we hardly know him at all, only his name, form, appearance, and a few outer mannerisms. His wife, after years of intimacy with him, may truly affirm that she knows him — and even then there are hidden provinces in his character that are probably more vast than the little she knows! Do yourself a big favor by reading and re-reading all four chapters of the book of Philippians as you read and study volume two. Repetitive reading may develop in each of us a greater capacity for seeing more of the truth that is here. Also, it will teach you directly more and more how to feed yourself from Scripture instead of being fed from someone else's spoon.

Enjoy the bread and don't forget to pass it on to feed more and more disciples!

Chapter 13

Characteristics of a Christian

"We are the circumcision, which worship God in the spirit, and rejoice in Christ Jesus, and have no confidence in the flesh" (Philippians 3:3).

The book of Philippians is the most tender-toned book in the New Testament. In Chapter two, Paul has lavishly praised his friends in Christ. However, in these verses a red flag of warning goes up, and a severe indictment goes out. "Beware of the dogs; beware of the evil workers; beware of the concision." It is urgent that we note Paul's explanation for using such strong words as this. "For you it is safe," he says in verse one. The word "safe" ("a safeguard," one translation says) indicates a danger, and just how *serious* a danger is indicated by the next verses. Here is one of the great motives for a disciple-maker. He disciples others because of concern for their spiritual safety, as well as their maximum productivity. The salvation of souls and *the safety of the saved* — these are masterful motives for maximum investment in making disciples.

There is no mincing of words here. Note that the seriousness of the warning is highlighted by the repeated use of the word "beware," which means to "be watchful." The repetition of this word is like the repeated blows of a gavel, signaling for attention. Danger was threatening his beloved Philippian brothers and sisters, and Paul sounds a clear warning. The language is vigorous and picturesque. Let's state another principle here: Sometimes incisive and bold warnings are necessary if true Christian love is to be expressed. "Beware of the dogs," Paul says. This is like a giant sign in a front yard that says, "Beware the Bad Dog." What suggestiveness there is in that figure! One of the most familiar sights in eastern cities is the sight of herds of dogs which prowl about without a home and without an owner, feeding on the trash and filth of the streets, fighting among themselves and attacking the passersby. Their home was the streets, and their food was trash. So Paul is not thinking of a house pet here, but of a large, savage, ugly scavenger dog. Now that is how the Jew thought about the Gentile. He was a dog. He had no home privileges in God. He was a homeless outcast religiously. He lived in the streets, as it were, and he fed on the crumbs which were thrown out from the more favored nation's table. The Jew was the home child; the Gentile was the creature of the gutter.

But now, Paul borrows their illustration and reverses the application of it. "The truth is," Paul says, "The Jews are living on the outer edges of reality. They magnify religious ceremonies and ordinances and institutions, but never press through them to truly find God." He turns to the Jews and says, "In reality, you are in the streets. You are the dogs. You are moving in the narrow channels of religious ceremonies and observances when you might be living in the spacious liberty of a spiritual faith." Beware of the dogs!

Then he adds," Beware of the evil workers!" You see, Paul's steps were constantly hounded by certain Jews (called Judaizers) who tried to bring Christians back into the bondage of ceremonial legalism. The people in question were *church-workers*! They thought of themselves as doers of good, but Paul viewed them as "evil workers" because they were reducing the Christian life to a legalistic system of dos and don'ts. The play on words which Paul uses in this verse reminds me of Martin Luther when he referred to the Pope as "Your hellishness" instead of "your holiness." Let's state an important principle at this point: Any person who aggressively teaches or promotes a works-salvation, while working for salvation himself, is an *evil worker*. So, while preaching and promoting and practicing what *he* regards as *good* works, he is actually preaching, practicing, and promoting evil works. In II Corinthians, Paul referred to them as "false apostles, deceitful workers, transforming themselves into apostles of Christ" (11:13). Paul says, "Beware of them if you value your full liberty in Christ!"

Then he says, "Beware of the circumcision!" There is a stinging play on words here. Circumcision was the Old Testament sign and seal of the covenant between God and His people. But Paul says that it had now lost its meaning to the Jews and amounted to nothing more than a "concision," a mere mutilating of the flesh. So he warns the Philippian Christians to beware of those who imagine that by merely curbing the flesh they can become heirs to a spiritual kingdom. Someone perceptively said that these Judaizers were inviting men to Christ with a Bible in one hand and a knife in the other! There is in these verses a solemn and urgent warning to today's Christian against a mere external faith which depends so much on outward ordinance and form.

But, in order that he does not leave them with a mere negative warning, Paul then unfolds the true life of the child of God, the individual who enjoys the rich life and fellowship of God's family circle. He now tells them what true circumcision is. It is the using of the knife of conviction and conversion on the heart instead of the flesh. It is spiritual rather than physical. He says, "We are the circumcision — we are the true Jews, we are God's chosen people today" — and then he gives three characteristics of a Christian. "We are the circumcision, who worship God in the spirit, and rejoice in Christ Jesus, and have no confidence in the flesh." I would like to invite you to explore with me these three characteristics of a true Christian. In actual experience, the order of the three clauses of verse three is reversed, so this is the way I will treat them.

HIS REPUDIATION OF THE FLESH

First, that person is a true Christian who repudiates any hope in himself. He has no confidence in the flesh. The first characteristic of a Christian is that he has realized that he cannot save himself and has then turned from himself in self distrust. "We have no confidence in the flesh." What does that mean? One of the best ways to interpret it is by performing a little mental exercise with the word "flesh." Take the word "flesh" and reverse the letters of it — "h-s-e-l-f." Then remove the "h," and you have left the four letters "s-e-l-f." All through the Letters of Paul, the "flesh" stands for self — the self that seeks to justify itself, that even endeavors to sanctify itself, that is always fussily trying to win men for God, but has never learned to be submerged beneath the mighty tide of God's Holy Spirit. The flesh may be wicked, it may be cultured, it may be polished, it may be educated, it may be civilized, it may be decent and honorable, it may be smooth, it may be religious, but it is repugnant and intolerable to God.

The word "flesh" stands for all that a man is and achieves apart from the Spirit of God. It is defined by all the list of things which follow in verses 4-6, things in which Paul trusted before he became a Christian, things such as religious ceremony, Jewish ancestry, social standing, personal prestige and moral attainments. In none of these things does a Christian put confidence as he stands before God. He realizes his helplessness, his utter unworthiness, his sin, and he knows that there is nothing in him that is acceptable to God. Every true Christian has seen that there is no grounds for confidence in the flesh, or in himself. In fact, he knows that everything about him in the flesh is repulsive to God.

This is what Alexander Whyte, the great Christian and marvelous Scottish preacher, meant when he said, "I am the worst man in Edinburgh." He had seen the "flesh" as it appears to God. This is also what the holy John Bunyan, author of *Pilgrim's Progress*, meant when he said "I feel that I am Cain who slew his brother, Esau who despised his birthright and Judas who betrayed his Lord, all rolled into one." When Martin Luther saw the true condition of his self-life, he cried out in despair, "Oh, my sins, my sins!" When a man is truly awakened before God to see himself, he can put no confidence in the flesh.

I like the way another translation puts it. "We have confidence, but not in the flesh!" "We have confidence." I love the assurance in those three words. Many times the Bible says, "We know." For example, "We know that our sins are forgiven for His name's sake." "We know," we have confidence, but not in the flesh. "We know that all things work together for good. . . " "We know," we have confidence, but not in the flesh. "We know that if our earthly house of this tabernacle be dissolved, we have a building of God, an house not made with hands, eternal in the heavens." "We know," we have confidence, but not in the flesh. Our confidence is born out of our faith in, and fellowship with, the Lord. "We have confidence, but not in the flesh."

HIS RELIANCE IN FAITH

Secondly, that person is a true Christian who relies on Jesus Christ alone. He glories only in Jesus Christ. "We rejoice in Christ Jesus." Dr. A. T. Robertson said, "The word "rejoice" belongs to Paul's "triumphant mood." It is the theme of Philippians. It occurs in one form or another some sixteen times in this brief letter. In this verse, the word means to "boast;" "we boast in Christ Jesus." The Jews also had their boast. They gloried in external things--in religious ritual and ceremony. But Christians find their only boast in Jesus Christ. He Himself is the Christian's crown of rejoicing. In Him we make our boast. We glory, directly and immediately, in Christ Jesus our Lord. In Galatians 6:14, Paul said "God forbid that I should glory , save in the cross of our Lord Jesus Christ." We may not be able to glory in our circumstances, our friends, or our prospects, but we can always rejoice in Jesus Christ. The supreme question for a professing Christian is, Do you really glory in Jesus Christ? Is He your boast and your pride? Is following Him your highest ideal? Do you talk about Jesus when you are with your friends? Is your heart drawn to Him like a needle attracted to a magnetic pole?

In this brief phrase, we have one of the very best definitions of faith man has ever known. Sometimes the impression is given that faith is a magical something that we exercise at one moment and thus we enter the kingdom of God, and that settles it. But Christian faith simply means that we glory, we boast, we rejoice now and always in Jesus Christ and in Him alone. Faith means that we have found in Christ the clue to everything that is worthwhile, and we have thus shifted the center of gravity in our lives away from self and onto Christ. "We glory in Jesus Christ." Faith echoes the words of Edward Mote:

"My hope is built on nothing less

Than Jesus' blood and righteousness;

I dare not trust the sweetest frame,

But wholly lean on Jesus' name.

His oath, His covenant, His blood,

Support me in the 'whelming flood;

When all around my soul gives way,

He then is all my hope and stay.

On Christ, the solid Rock, I stand,

All other ground is sinking sand."

HIS RELATIONSHIP IN FELLOWSHIP

A Christian is a person who lives in an adoring relationship with God through Christ. He worships God in the spirit as the continuing expression of his faith, love and gratitude. "We worship God in the Spirit." Our worship is not a ceremonial act, not the curbing of the flesh, nor the eating of a wafer or the burning of a candle. "We worship God in the Spirit." Ours is a spiritual worship, an ongoing spiritual relationship. Every form and ceremony, every posture, every outward means of grace, every ordinance must bring us into the very Holy of Holies, into the "secret place of the Most High, to dwell under the shadow of the Almighty." Even the Bible must not be our goal; it must be a street through which we pass to the Lord.

In I Corinthians 3:16, there is a question that throws light on this phrase. It says, "Know ye not that ye are the temple of God?" I Corinthians 6:19 adds, "Know ye not that your body is the temple of the Holy Ghost, who dwells in you?" In the first reference, the pronoun is plural, referring to the entire local church at Corinth. In chapter six, the pronoun is singular, referring to the individual believer. What a great word that is! Mark it well. If I am a temple, a church, then the worshiper is within. If this body is a cathedral, then what sort of worship service is going on within at this moment? Is the Holy of Holies dark and silent, or is a service proceeding? Are you genuinely worshiping in the Spirit, or is a mere form taking place?

You know what kind of service was observed in Paul's temple, don't you? We have several little glimpses in his letters, as if we were permitted to look into his temple through an open doorway. He held daily services — in fact, continuous services, in his temple. The fire was always burning on the altar of his heart. Listen to his words. "I give thanks without ceasing." That is part of the worship which proceeded in the inner temple of Paul's life. Not only during my morning devotions, or at vespers, or at mid-week prayer service, or on Sunday at church, but without ceasing! Inside that temple the worshiping spirit daily rehearsed the Lord's mercies, and sent a continuous stream of praise to God. That is worship in the Spirit.

Or look at another glimpse of the service in Paul's inner temple. "I pray without ceasing." Inside the temple the spirit was always on its knees. Always! Yes, when Paul went from the quiet of the synagogue to the noise of the marketplace, his spirit did not change its position. It remained upon its knees. When Jesus of Nazareth passed from His baptism to the temptation then on to the marriage in Cana of Galilee, His spirit did not change; the service within the personal temple proceeded. The spirit remained in a posture of prayer. This is the glory of spiritual worship. We do not light a candle, or count a rosary, or kneel before an image. True worship does not need these crutches, for it takes place within.

Thus, when we pass into the shop, or the office, or the store, or the classroom, or the place of business, our soul can retain its reverence, and even in the commonplace we can be possessed by the consciousness of the presence of God. Throughout the day, the spirit in the temple can remain upon its knees, remembering that it is always in the presence of the eternal and holy God.

One more thing took place in the temple of the Apostle Paul. If I am a temple, then who is the priest? Why, I am! Jesus is the High Priest over the entire House of God, but I am my own priest before Him. "He hath made us .. priests unto God our Father" (Revelation 1:6). One of the tasks of the priest in the temple is to offer sacrifice unto God. What are we to sacrifice? What did Paul offer? Himself. "I am poured out upon the altar." In Phil. 2:17, he said, "I am offered upon the sacrifice and service of your faith." He offered himself as a ceaseless sacrifice to his God.

These are the temple services of the Apostle Paul. Thanksgiving! Supplication! Sacrifice! This is the nature of the Christian life. The Christian life is a glorious life in which we constantly "worship God in the spirit." It is interesting to note that the words "worship" and "service" are sometimes used interchangeably in the New Testament. For example, in Romans 12:1, we read, "I beseech you, therefore, brethren, by the mercies of God, that ye present your bodies a living sacrifice, holy, acceptable unto God, which is your reasonable service (worship)." The surrender of yourself in active service for Christ then is an act of worship. Thus, every service you render in the Spirit is an act of worship.

These, then, are the characteristics of a Christian. Each reader should do a check-up on himself right now. Have I given up all hope of salvation in myself? Is my faith fully exercised in Christ alone? Do I regularly worship God in my spirit, and in *His Spirit*? Perhaps you have just realized that you are not really a Christian. What are you to do? Confess your sins directly to God, admitting everything and hiding nothing. Remember that Jesus Christ has loved you personally and unconditionally, and that He died on the cross of Calvary for you and your sins. Then He arose from the dead to justify you. He says that if you will trust Him and Him alone for salvation, He will forgive your sins, give you the gift of eternal life, and live in your heart. Trust Him now; trust Him totally. Then, confess Him openly with your lips and your life. And keep the flame of love for Him burning on the altar of your heart.

Chapter 14

The Disciple-Maker's Final Balance Sheet

For we are the circumcision, which worship God in the spirit, and rejoice in Christ Jesus, and have no confidence in the flesh. Though I might also have confidence in the flesh. If any other man thinketh that he hath whereof he might trust in the flesh, I more: Circumcised the eighth day, of the stock of Israel, of the tribe of Benjamin, a Hebrew of the Hebrews; as touching the law, a Pharisee; Concerning zeal, persecuting the church; touching the righteousness which is in the law, blameless. But what things were gain to me, those I counted loss for Christ. Yea doubtless, and I count all things but loss for the excellency of the knowledge of Christ Jesus my Lord: for whom I have suffered the loss of all things, and do count them but dung, that I may win Christ, And be found in him, not having mine own righteousness, which is of the law, but that which is through the faith of Christ, the righteousness which is of God by faith: That I may know him, and the power of his resurrection, and the fellowship of his sufferings, being made conformable unto his death; If by any means I might attain unto the resurrection of the dead (Philippians 3:3-11).

A little boy came into the living room of his home one day, and he did not know that his pastor had come for a visit in their home. His mother was seated across the room, and the pastor was seated off to the side, out of the boy's line of vision. The boy came rushing into the room, and he was carrying a little mouse by the tail. The mouse was lifeless and badly mangled. The boy exclaimed, "Momma, guess what I did! I hit him with a broomstick, and rolled my tricycle over him, and then I stomped on him with my foot." Then the boy noticed that his mother was looking past him to someone else in the room. He turned and saw the preacher, suddenly became pious, and added, *"And then the Lord took him home!"* Paul clearly warns the Philippian Christians against those who mix religion and meanness. "Beware of the dogs," he says, and he isn't talking about nice household pets. The dogs he has in mind are the cruel, vicious, snapping, snarling, barking, biting deadly roving packs of pariah dogs, scavenger dogs, which may be commonly seen in villages throughout the Middle East.

Don't fool yourself. Some of the meanest people on earth may be *religious* people. Paul describes them as "dogs," and "evil workers," and "the concision," those who mutilate both the truth and the people they would lead. He is speaking here of the legalistic Judaizers, who insist on diluting grace with works and thus rendering grace ineffective and powerless. And the Judaizers were mean in doing it. Distemper and mean disposition are not new in the area of religion. Every "religious" group has its fair share of them, and they may show up at any time in anyone, if that person is not restrained and conditioned by the grace of God and a consistent walk with Christ.

A Quaker man was milking his cow. The cow suddenly lifted a hind foot and placed it down squarely in the milk pail and into the milk. The Quaker patiently lifted the hoof out of the milk and replaced it in its proper place. The cow repeated the unpleasant action. Again, the Quaker replaced the hoof. A little later, the cow did it again. The Quaker sighed and repeated the distasteful action. *The cow did it again.* The Quaker said firmly to the cow, "Thou dost know that I am a Quaker, and I would not hurt thee, but if thou continuest in this course, *tomorrow I will sell thee to a Southern Baptist, and he will beat the devil out of thee!"* You see, man's nature has within it the capability of incredible anger and bad disposition, and the realm of religion often excites these very elements in human nature.

No wonder a true Christian "has no confidence in the flesh" (the uncontrolled, unrestrained self-life of the individual)!

In our text, Paul uses an illustration from the business world. He constructs a business man's Balance Sheet. He draws up a "Profit and Loss Statement" as if he were a practicing merchant writing a record of his assets and liabilities. The passage opens with Paul asserting what seems to be an incredible boast. He says, "If any man could boast in the flesh (self-achievement in religion, in this case), I am that man. If any other man thinks that he might trust in the flesh, I have more self-achievement to boast of than he does." The term "any other man" is major emphasis in that sentence, which means it is a loud shout from the page. So Paul calls on humanity to present a champion to compete with him in religious self-achievement. Bring out *"any other man" — your very best*, he says, and I will over-match him in religious achievement. "You bring out the greatest legal champion of religion and morality this world has ever known, and he does not have the boast that I can make. I take second place to no man in my religious performance in the flesh," Paul declares, and he was surely right. If anybody could trust in the flesh, and boast of his accomplishment, Paul was that man. So the passage becomes a contrast between what religious human beings can accomplish in their own efforts to make themselves presentable to God (which Paul finally calls "dung"), and the provision God has made for all men, religious or otherwise, in Christ (which Paul finally calls "the supreme advantage"). The resulting "Profit and Loss Statement" becomes one of the "high water marks" of Christian revelation in the New Testament. It has been a favorite passage of mine for over forty years.

Paul brings before us a list of "gilt-edged securities" from his noble performance in a noble religion, Judaism, and honestly presents them to our attention. Though he boasted in the flesh before he became a Christian, his boast was based on fact. Look carefully at the developments in this passage.

PAUL REVIEWS HIS RELIGIOUS ADVANTAGES

First, the Apostle lists the religious advantages he had and had created as a Jew who practiced his religion with incredible zeal. The statement, "If any other man thinketh that he hath whereof he might trust in the flesh, I more," triggers his mind to recite the list of advantages he had as a practicing Jew. There are seven items in the list, and they comprise a great study of religious privilege and achievement.

Paul divides these advantages into two categories. The two categories could be labeled, *"RECEIVED Advantages"* and *"ACHIEVED Advantages."* The "received advantages" were those religious benefits which Paul had *obtained from his parents*, or derived from his ancestral background. Even today, we hear such claims as, "My father was a deacon," or "My mother was a Sunday School teacher," or "I was practically raised in church." These are "received advantages."

The "achieved advantages" were those religious benefits which Paul had *attained by his performance* in the noble religion of Judaism. One set of benefits came from his *ancestry*, while the other came from his own *action*. One came from his *pedigree*, the other from his *performance*. Today, the claim is often made, "I've always tried to be a good person," or "I try to live right, and not hurt anybody." Supposedly, these are achieved advantages (though the very sound of them is shallow and weak). It is hard for a true Christian to imagine offering these "advantages" to God as the hope of salvation, but the practice is overwhelmingly common.

Back in the first half of the twentieth century, there was a great British man of finance named Leo Page. Page was a banker and a great Christian gentleman. When he retired in the middle 1940s, he wrote a lengthy poem about his life as a financier. The poem is sprinkled liberally with spiritual insights. The closing part of the poem includes these words,

> *"When I advance with faltering feet,*
> *To show my final Balance Sheet. . . "*

When Leo Page died on September 2, 1951, his obituary was printed in the *London Times*. His long poem was included in the obituary, and one of his friends was quoted in the last line: "You may believe that his account was in order." Project yourself ahead to the Final Hearing. If you are aware of your failings, you know that you will come "with faltering feet," though you stand "clothed in Christ's righteousness alone, faultless to stand before the throne." That is a matter of salvation, but now your performance as a Christian is to be evaluated. You will surely come to that moment "with faltering feet." Our text is Paul's salvation balance sheet. Now let's join Paul as he recites his previous "advantages" in Judaism.

Advantage Number One (a *received* advantage): "I was circumcised the eighth day." That is quite enough for a Jew to create a boast in the flesh. So his life began with the right *ritual*. A proselyte to Judaism was circumcised whenever he became a Jew. An Ishmaelite was circumcised at the time of his thirteenth birthday. But a person of full Jewish parentage was circumcised on the eighth day. Circumcision was the sign and seal of the covenant between God and Abraham (Genesis 17:9-14). Paul is saying, "Though others may get the advantage in other ways, I have a birthright to this seal of the covenant. I am a full-blooded and true-born Jew, with full rights and privileges mine by birth."

As an aside, note the term, "the eighth day." Again, we are confronted with one of the millions of tiny splendors of Scripture. Why the eighth day? Is that a mere arbitrary choice? No, it certainly is not! The "K" factor, the clotting factor, in the blood of a male human being is never at the level in the rest of his life that it reaches on the eighth day of his life. It is at its most favorable level for blood-letting on that day. An Original Physician dictated this procedure from His infinite and perfect medical knowledge! So Paul begins his list with a grand assertion of a ritual that reveals him to be a fully privileged Jew.

Advantage Number Two (a *received* advantage): "I am of the stock of Israel." I not only have a ritualistic advantage, I also have a *religious* advantage, Paul says. I wasn't grafted in as so many others have been. I was of the original "stock" of Israel. And notice the name Paul uses for his nation — not "Jacob," the original name, and the name used for the carnal and fleshly nation. No, he uses the name of the nation that comes after Jacob's transformation into a man in relationship with God, "Israel." At first, he was called "Jacob," which means "supplanter," or "cheat." Then, God changed his name to "Israel," which means "Prince with God." I was of the very stock of Israel, Paul declares.

Advantage Number Three (a *received* advantage): "I was of the tribe of Benjamin." The tribe of Benjamin was the smallest of the tribes of Israel (Psalm 68:27 called it "little Benjamin"), and it offered exclusive privileges. The tribe of Benjamin provided the best warriors to the armies of Israel, and the Benjamites usually led those armies into battle. Benjamin was one of the two favorite sons of Jacob's favorite wife, Rachel. The first king of Israel, Saul, was of the tribe of Benjamin, and Saul of Tarsus, the writer of our text, was named after him. The tribe of Benjamin remained loyal with Judah when the other tribes betrayed their Jewish heritage and created the division of the kingdom. The Benjamites were renowned for stern courage and persistent faithfulness. "I am of the tribe of Benjamin," Paul says. Not only did he have the advantages of proper ritual, and proper religion, but now he adds the advantage of proper *relationship*.

Advantage Number Four (a *received* advantage): "I am a Hebrew of Hebrews" (the KJV says, "a Hebrew of the Hebrews," but there is no article, "the," in the original text). So Paul could also add the advantage of *race* to his other supposed advantages. Neither Paul's father nor mother had an ounce of Gentile blood in them. "I am a blend of perfect Jewish ancestry. I am a 'blue-blood,' a Jew of the highest pedigree. I am a Hebrew produced out of the conjoining of Hebrews; there is no contamination in my bloodline." When the Gospel of John points out the spiritual lineage of one born of God, it says that he is born "not of bloods" (John 1:13). The plural word is significant. It means that though you may amalgamate in your history an ancestry of thoroughbred religious parents, that ancestry is of no worth before God in producing eternal salvation. The grace of God does not flow in a human bloodstream, or in the joining of pedigreed bloodstreams. If anyone had the right to hope in his ancestry, that man was the Apostle Paul, so it is crucial to see how he discounts that ancestry as having any vital part in his eternal salvation.

Rehearse again Paul's received advantages, the advantages he obtained from his parents: the advantages of ritual, religion, relationship, and race. Now, Paul lists his achieved advantages, the advantages he attained by his performance.

Advantage Number Five (an *achieved* advantage): "As touching the law, I was a Pharisee." No modern mind can possibly appreciate the advantage that this would have given a first-century Jew. Paul now adds to the list the advantage of *rank*. We often misread the Pharisees through our ignorance. We are often quite unfair to them, seeing only the worst side because of our conditioning. We are not objective enough to see that they had great strengths as well as glaring and growing weaknesses. Anyone thinking of a Pharisee in the New Testament world would have greatly admired him for his devotion and discipline. First-century Jews might never have viewed the Pharisees as bad, but we see them only as bad. They were probably the best moral people who had ever lived, as far as legal and religious morality can go.

The Pharisees were the very strict, conservative, fundamentalist Jews. They wanted to be clearly distinguished from the Sadducees, the religious liberals of Judaism. The Sadducees did not believe in the supernatural world, or in angels, or in the resurrection, or in heaven or hell. So they were "sad-you-see"! The Pharisees put great trust in their own immaculate religious performances. A Pharisee might stand before a mirror, think of his morality and religion, and say, "Oh, I'm 'fair-I-see'". And they were quite commendable in their dedication and discipline. I think of myself as a conservative Christian, and I even admit to being a fundamentalist, though that word is usually used very unjustly to caricature and smear conservative Christians in an ignorant and abusive way. But so was Paul — *a Jewish fundamentalist!* Friends, we must be very careful in taking pride in our theological stance. The Pharisees were the custodians of the Jewish law, and the keepers of the Jewish nation. They had divided the law into the most meticulous parts, and attempted to keep it perfectly at every point. They were apparently in good faith except for their decline into religious pride, which such religion breeds. Paul was a Pharisee (see Galatians 1:13-14 for a staggering statement of his achievement as a Pharisee), and according to Acts 23:6, his father was also a Pharisee! So he had compounded cause for boasting in the flesh.

Advantage Number Six (an *achieved* advantage): "Concerning zeal, I was persecuting the church." Now he adds the advantage of his *record* as a zealous Jew. Paul says, "I was so intent on protecting and defending my understanding of faith and religion that I tried to sledgehammer to death all of those I thought of as God's enemies, and I thought I was doing God, myself, and everyone else a favor in trying to stamp out the Christian movement." Paul later said to the Romans, "I bear them record that they have a zeal of God, but not according to knowledge" (Romans 10:3). His description of religious enthusiasts without Christ was merely an echo of his own stance before he became a believer in Christ. He himself had a zeal for God — but not according to knowledge. Listen to his own words as he later described what he did. He writes to the Galatians, "You have heard of my lifestyle in times past in the Jews' religion ('Ioudaism,' or Judaism), how that beyond measure ('huperbole,' literally, 'throwing beyond,' or excessively) I persecuted (see Acts 7 & 9) the church of God (he now sees the real nature of his deed, as being against God and His Church!), and wasted ('ravaged, destroyed,' Acts 9:21) it. And profited ('advanced, progressed'; the word is an engineering term, and it literally means 'to strike forward, to cut forward,' like a corps of engineers chopping their way through a thick forest. It combines the ideas of intense effort, determination, and zeal) in the Jews' religion ('Judaism') above many my equals in mine own nation, being more exceedingly zealous of the traditions of my fathers" (Galatians 1:13-14). Read these words several times, and in several translations. Get the "feel" and the meaning of them. Listen to the natural outcome of this religious zeal in the life of Paul: "As for Saul, he made havoc of the church, entering into every house, and haling men and women committed them to prison" (Acts 8:3). Paul was a quite legalistic and fundamentalistic Jew, and religious legalism always tends toward fanaticism!

A fundamentalist and legalistic Christian "hated cigarettes and cigarette smoking." In fact, he hated smoking so badly that, when he saw any person smoking, he would rush up to him, jerk the cigarette out of his mouth, throw it to the ground, stomp on it with his foot, and run away. Well, he finally died of foot cancer! One can easily see how supposed religious advantages are actually extreme disadvantages — and this is true of all religion!

Advantage Number Seven (the last one, an *achieved* advantage): "As touching the righteousness which is in the law, I was blameless." So he had the supposed advantage of personal *righteousness*, and his performance was truly remarkable. The word "blameless" means "uncensored." Imagine this claim: "I stood uncensored before God and His holy law." Paul sounds here just like the rich young ruler (Matthew 19:16-22). When Jesus stated the social demands of the law of God, the young man answered, "All these things have I observed from my youth up; what lack I yet?" Can you personally imagine making such an extravagant moral claim as that while standing face to face with Incarnate Holiness — with God Himself?! But Paul, who was a fierce religionist, makes the same claim as he finishes his list of supposed personal advantages in morality and religion.

His list is now complete. He recites his received advantages — those of his ritual, his religion, his relationship, and his race. Then he rehearses his achieved advantages — those of his rank, his record, and his righteousness. Renowned writer Mark Twain wrote a story entitled, "Seven Characters In Search of a Plot." Here, we see seven religious "virtues" in search of eternal life. But Paul shows that the quest for eternal life was fruitless if pursued through religious beliefs and practices, no matter how good they are. Religion, man's attempt to make himself presentable before God, must be replaced by true relationship with God, relationship which develops into a true romance between the human heart and the Eternal Lover.

PAUL RENOUNCES HIS RELIGIOUS ADVANTAGES

Next, Paul repudiates those supposed advantages in which he had placed his entire hope and trust before he met Christ. What a monumental reversal is taking place right before our eyes! He begins to juggle his previous balance sheet. The things he once saw as assets, he now recognizes as liabilities. And the things he saw as liabilities before, he now sees as assets. His debits have become credits, and his credits are now debits! What a staggering turn-around, and especially for a full-blooded, practicing Jew!

Note his words with great care. *"But what things were gain to me, those I counted loss for Christ. Yea doubtless, and I count all things but loss for the excellency of the knowledge of Christ Jesus my Lord: for whom I have suffered the loss of all things, and do count them but dung"* (verses 7 & 8). "What things were gain to me" — now, his previous evaluation has been changed. The past tense of the verb includes all of Paul's history before he met Jesus Christ. The word "gain" is plural ("gains"), packaging together as one bundle all of those previous supposed advantages we have discussed. "Those I counted loss for Christ." The word "count" occurs three times in these next verses — once in verse seven, and twice in verse eight. In verse seven, it is a perfect tense verb. It means that at one point on the time line, something happened that caused him to totally reverse his Balance Sheet, and he came to count as loss everything he had seen before as a gain. And the perfect tense verb means that his new evaluation is irreversible! But in verse eight, the verb is a present tense: "I am continuing to count all those things but loss." It is as if Paul said, "In light of what happened in one great transforming moment, and in light of what I have continued to discover since then about the Person I have put in the place of all those supposed gains, I continue counting everything else but loss." This is an incredible testimony from an intellectual Jew who had previously practiced his Jewish religion with immeasurable zeal and earnestness.

The past tense verb of verse seven, "I counted those things loss for Christ," refers to Paul's *conversion*. In that conversion, a crisis of reevaluation occurred. All my previous advantages were instantaneously canceled, Paul cries. A man asked his income tax adviser, "Can I deduct my wife's beauty treatment from my taxes?" "Why, no," answered his adviser in surprise, "whatever gave you the impression that you could deduct your wife's beauty treatment?" "Well, it was a total loss!" the man retorted. Even so, Paul now reports as a total loss all the religious and moral performances he had practiced before Christ entered his life. The present tense verbs of verse eight, "I count all things but loss," and "I count them but dung," refers to Paul's continuing evaluation, as the process of transformation progresses.

What happened to this man? Negatively, he suddenly saw all those previous supposed advantages in the blazing light of the only thing that really counts. There is a great illustration of this text in the dramatic shipwreck story in the twenty-seventh chapter of the Book of Acts. The word that is translated "loss" three times in our text is never used elsewhere in the Bible except in that story (Acts 27), where it occurs twice more. Recall the story. Paul is on his way to Rome to go on trial for his life. He has appealed to Caesar, and he is being transported to Rome by ship. Trying to complete the trip before storm season on the Mediterranean, they were caught in an extremely severe storm, a storm which lasted for fourteen days and nights. That ship became like a cork in a bathtub with someone slapping the water. I heard about a ship that sailed the high seas with a cargo of yo-yo's on board. It ran into a storm -- and sank forty-two times! The ship Paul was traveling on was in that kind of danger. The storm was so ferocious that the crew belted the ship to keep it from breaking to pieces.

The ship was carrying a cargo of wheat, the reason for the ship's journey. That wheat was considered a "gain" to the owner of the wheat, a gain to every crew member aboard the ship, and it was a potential gain to anyone who negotiated to buy and sell that wheat. However, it was only and always regarded as a "gain" because there was no issue any greater than the profit of that wheat. But the moment life and death became the issue, they threw that cargo of wheat overboard as if it were totally worthless! That which had been regarded as nothing but gain previously was reckoned instantly to be worthless in comparison to the value of life itself. And no lengthy thought was necessary to make that reckoning!

Paul made a similar reckoning here. He had discovered that religion was like a vine (the religious adherent, the "believer") fastening itself to a dead tree (the religion). An actual vine attached itself to the dead limb of a tree and clung there. But a storm broke the limb off the trunk of the tree, leaving the vine lying on the ground without support. The limb may be a religious institution, or a religious ritual, or a religious practice, or a favorite minister, but these things will collapse and leave the soul without eternal support.

Here stands a man before God. He draws himself up smugly in the pride of his own character and performance and announces to himself, "I am quite safe and invulnerable. If anyone has reason to boast in his standing, I have such a reason." You see, he has never previously seen the true nature and responsibility of this position. That accurate awareness requires a miracle, a miracle which is called "conviction" (see John 16:7-11). But now, that miracle has happened for this man. His eyes have been opened to eternal reality. The issues of life, death, and eternity have come home to his mind, heart, and soul with their proper force. Previously, he could be superficial in his evaluations, though he did not realize how shallow his evaluations were. But now, as Thomas

Carlyle once said, "Through the cobwebs of life, death and eternity sat glaring at me!" What a revolution occurs, what a transformation happens, in such a moment! In that moment, Paul says, "I packaged up all the things I had earlier thought to be gains, and I threw them all overboard on account of Christ." My friend, if this has not happened to you, you need to have a good, long, accurate, absorbing look at Jesus!

George Regas, in a book with a strange title, *Kiss Yourself and Hug the World*, writes, "There is a moment in Leonard Bernstein's modern opera, MASS, with which I identify in the most profound way. The priest celebrating the mass puts on one priestly vestment after another, one elegant robe on top of another. Then the priest staggers under the weight of all that tradition. There is a sense of violence in the scene, as if all that religiosity is about to destroy him. Finally the priest tears off all the vestments and stands in his blue jeans and a T-shirt before the altar. He sings, 'Look at me. There is nothing but me under this.'" This is the kind of transaction Paul makes in our text. And forever after, he could never understand why anyone in his right mind would want to go back to the old way of religious tradition and bondage. I agree. Would a modern Chinese woman who has been set free from the traditions of bound feet and obsolete ways return to their discomfort and deformity? Paul here repudiates his previous supposed advantages — because he has found something infinitely better.

PAUL REPLACES HIS PREVIOUS ADVANTAGES

Finally, the Apostle Paul *replaces* his supposed previous advantages with Christ Himself. "Yea, doubtless, and I count ..." This is a present tense verb. Christian, are you doing this right now? Look at the Balance Sheet of your life. How much value do you give to anything else? Does Jesus Christ totally determine the value system of your life? Is everything else basically worthless when compared to Christ? Be very careful at this point. Imagine yourself giving up all possessions and relationships in a moment, and see if Christ alone would be enough in that moment. Have you abandoned "all things" (verse eight) — all good things (your securities, your possessions, your relationships, your morality, etc.), and all bad things (your sins, mistakes, and failures) — and determined that Jesus is really all you have and all you need? Note Paul's reason for making such as exchange: "On account of the excellency of knowing Christ Jesus my Lord." Here is the supreme advantage of life! And these words were written by a man who could marshal a list of the very best advantages man can find outside of Christ!

Other translations may help us understand the magnificence of these words. H. C. G. Moule speaks of "the surpassingness of knowing Christ." Another speaks of "the superiority of knowing Christ." *The New American Standard Bible* combines these ideas into "the surpassing value of knowing Christ." *The Amplified Bible* translates it, "I count everything as loss compared to the possession of the priceless privilege — the overwhelming preciousness — of knowing Christ Jesus my Lord, and of progressively becoming more deeply and intimately acquainted with Him, of perceiving and recognizing and understanding Him more fully and clearly."

At this point, let me share with you the live, intense, moving translation of our entire text by Eugene Peterson in his *The Message* paraphrase: "I can list what many might think are impressive credentials. You know my pedigree: a legitimate birth, circumcised on the eighth day; an Israelite from the elite tribe of Benjamin; a strict and devout adherent to God's law; a fiery defender of the purity of my religion, even to the point of persecuting Christians; a meticulous observer of everything set down in God's law Book. The very credentials these people are waving around as something special, I'm tearing up and throwing out with the trash — along with everything else I used to take credit for. And why? Because of Christ. Yes, all the things I once thought were so important are gone from my life. Compared to the high privilege of knowing Christ Jesus as my Master, firsthand, everything I once thought I had going for me is insignificant — dog dung. I've dumped it all in the trash so that I could embrace Christ and be embraced by him. I didn't want some petty, inferior brand of righteousness that comes from keeping a list of rules when I could get the robust kind that comes from trusting Christ — God's righteousness."

I think that any honest reader would see that Paul has crossed a "Grand Canyon" of experience and relationship, and his life has been absolutely turned right side up! Well, dear friend, the same thing has happened to me! And to multitudes of others! A Great Divide has been crossed. We have left one bank of "the Rubicon" and stand solidly on the far side, and we are not even looking back! The glory of Christ is increasingly prepossessing us — in spite of ourselves and our many sins and failures! Jesus is increasingly becoming "all in all" to us. And we must confess that we find great pity in our hearts for the person who is still standing in the dung pile on the other side of this relationship.

This is what Paul had come to: *(1) A new perspective.* "The things I counted as gains, I have come to regard as losses. The things I once saw as losses, I now see as gains." *(2) A new position.* "My desire is to be found in Christ." Whether he is searched out by the day of living or the day of dying, the day of judgment, the day of eternity, the day of destiny, his one desire is to be found in Christ. *(3) A new possession.* "Not having my own righteousness, which is of the law, but that which is through the faith of Christ, the righteousness which is of God by faith." *(4) A new potential.* "That I may always get to know Christ better." Paul is like Christopher Columbus, landed on the beach of a continent, and not knowing how vast the interior is, but beginning to explore that limitless continent. "I have landed; now I want to thoroughly explore the interior. Every day I live, I want to know Christ better." Jesus is an infinite Person, and will require infinite study and infinite personal adjustments to adequately know Him. This is a task that might occupy all of eternity. Jesus is easily possessed at the introduction of the relationship, but His personality will require limitless exploration to get to fully know Him.

License your imagination, and picture this scene. See the grey light of pre-dawn on a certain day. Our focus is on a young Pharisee. He is wearing the clothing of his religious order. But he had dressed in the dark. You see, every man who thinks he can make himself acceptable to God has dressed in the dark. He is wearing the phylacteries, tiny boxes containing scripture texts, on his wrists and forehead. The broad borders of his robe are also covered with scripture texts. He wears the sacred cord that identifies him as a son of the law. He wears the inner "garment of zeal," and over that, a robe that appears spotless, "the righteousness of the law." Decked in all of this impressive finery, he thinks of himself as "blameless." Around the room are burnished mirrors, and as he considers his garments in the grey light, he imagines himself to be highly commendable and likely to stand an excellent chance to pass the Divine examination — both for this world, and the world to come. But remember, he has dressed in the dark. He can only think these garments to be presentable enough because the light has been so dim. If the light had been brighter, he would have detected all kinds of disqualifying blemishes in his covering.

While we stand gazing into this room, the dim grey light brightens into the morning, and in the light of its growing brightness, the young Pharisee beholds himself in the mirrors. As he examines himself in the growing light, he becomes increasingly distressed over what he sees. He notices a series of flaws in the "blameless" robe of his personal righteousness, and he takes it off and flings it away. Then he strips off the "garment of zeal," realizing that it is not as pure as he once thought it to be. Successively, he puts aside his Pharisaic dress, one garment at a time. As the revealing light shows how filthy his garments really are (Isaiah 64:6), he strips them off, and tramples them beneath his feet, refusing to trust in them any longer. He is horrified to think that if the Sun of Righteousness, Jesus, had not arisen (Malachi 4:2), he might have gone out into eternity and never known his mistake until he faced the Great White Throne, the place of condemnation for all lost people.

Now the soul has been stripped of all of its false trusts. It has been stripped of all dependence upon itself, its feelings, its good desires, its good ambitions, its prayers, its baptism, its church membership, its performance, its works, its character. Suddenly, in the light of desperate dependence, he sees Jesus, holding in His pierced hand a bright, clean robe of perfect righteousness, a robe woven on the looms of Heaven by the hands of Christ Himself. This is the perfect justification which He has purchased with His own hands, and which he now offers to the former Pharisee. In fact, this righteousness is offered to all men, whether "secular" sinners or "sacred" sinners, on the basis of faith. As we watch, the naked young former Pharisee (a "sacred" sinner) puts out his trembling hand and takes the perfect robe. As if assisted by an unseen Divine Hand, he is quickly clothed in this new garment. As this happens, Paul's soul echoes an old song of celebration which will never cease: "I will greatly rejoice in the Lord, my soul shall exult in my God: for He has clothed me with the garments of salvation, He has covered me with the robe of righteousness" (Isaiah 61:10).

> "My hope is built on nothing less,
> Than Jesus' blood and righteousness,
> I dare not trust the sweetest frame,
> But wholly lean on Jesus' Name.
> When He shall come with trumpet sound,
> O may I then in Him be found:
> Dressed in His righteousness alone,
> Faultless to stand before the throne.
> On Christ, the solid rock, I stand,
> All other ground is sinking sand."

Chapter 15

The Transforming Friendship

"That I may know Him" (Philippians 3:10a).

In a book that exposes a great man's great heart, the Apostle Paul is now permitting us to go with him into the innermost sanctuary of that heart, into the Holy of Holies of his very being. He is revealing to us the supreme passion of his life. He is letting us know what is his one great ambition. "That I may know Christ!" Of course, the working premise of this ambition is that Christ does not live way back in the remote centuries of a very distant past, but that he is alive and available today. Jesus is where you are, and you may meet Him and cultivate relationship with Him anytime and in any place.

Paul gave his greatest personal testimony when he said, "I know Whom I have believed, and am persuaded that He is able to keep that which I have committed unto Him against that day" (II Timothy 1:12). To know a person is much more than to merely know about that person. Knowing about Jesus has a measure of value, but only knowing Him in continual personal relationship has vitality. To know His gifts is good, but this is far more. To know His blessings is good, but this is far more. To know His comforts is good, but this is far more.

No true Christian can be put off by a doctrine about Christ, or by the Book about Christ, as crucially important as these benefits may be. No Christian can be satisfied with a hearsay or second-hand knowledge of Christ. The true Christian presses through all of these things like the vestibules of a building, passing from one to another, to stand in the Loving Presence of Christ Himself. John Greenleaf Whittier said it best in these lines:

> *"No fable old, no mythic lore*
> *No dream of bards and seers,*
> *No dead fact, stranded on the shore*
> *Of the oblivious years;*
> *But warm, sweet, tender, even yet*
> *A present help is He,*
> *And faith has still its Olivet,*
> *And love its Galilee."*

When Paul wrote the words of our text, he had already been a Christian for over thirty years! His longing was to know the mind and heart and love and friendship of Christ in an ever-enlarging degree. We say that Columbus discovered America, but not all of America is even yet discovered. Even if Columbus knew he had discovered a continent, he could have no idea of the vastness of that continent that would need exploration and continuing discovery. And so it is with our exploration of the infinite Person of Jesus.

Paul also knew that this knowing of Christ had a high price-tag attached to it. In verses 7 and 8, he said, "What things were gain to me, I counted loss for Christ. Yea doubtless, and I count all things but loss for the excellency of the knowledge of Christ Jesus my Lord: for whom I have suffered the loss of all things, and do count them but dung, that I may win Christ." Author Oscar Wilde once referred to "a man who knows the price of everything and the value of nothing." But Paul is a man who paid the price of knowing Christ because he knew the incredible value of knowing Christ. In fact, He decided on life's greatest value, Jesus, at any price, because he recognized that the Value is always greater than the price. The value is so great that the price is not even considered.

The typical Christian vocabulary is replete with such terms as "accepting Christ," "believing in Christ," "trusting Christ," and "knowing Christ." But what does "knowing Christ" mean? Many relational metaphors could be used: teacher-disciple; master-slave; father-son; commanding officer-soldier; coach-athlete; king-subject; bridegroom-bride, etc. Each relationship presents a marvelous dimension of the Christian life, but there is one which contains the richest dimensions of all. *That is the relationship of friend and friend.* The Weymouth Translation of Romans 6:23 says, "God's free gift is the Life of the Ages bestowed upon us in Christ Jesus our Lord." Of course, the gift is Eternal Life, but it can be best understood as the gift of the everlasting personal friendship of Jesus with the believing heart. In fact, Jesus Himself defined Eternal Life in these words, "This is life eternal, that they may know Thee the only true God, and Jesus Christ whom Thou hast sent." So Eternal Life could be defined as knowing God through friendship with Jesus Christ. In this sense, Christianity is the acceptance of the gift of the friendship of Jesus. "That I may know Him" is simply the expression of desire for a deeper friendship with Jesus. So we are examining today "The Transforming Friendship," the friendship between a sensitive and spiritual Christian and the Great Friend, Jesus.

THE GIFT OF FRIENDSHIP

First, we will consider the *gift* of this transforming friendship.

A Gracious Gift

Friendship between Jesus and any human being is an absolute gift of grace provided solely out of the gracious goodwill of Jesus Himself. Jesus said, "I have called you my friends." The giver of the friendship is Christ Himself. No sinner could establish this friendship without the Divine initiative and permission of Jesus. Paul South said, "A true friend is the gift of God, and only He who made hearts can unite them." This is certainly true. Jesus as a True Friend is a gift of God, and His friendship is certainly a gratuity from God.

This allows us to see our only proper attitude toward Him. The proper attitude to a good gift is acceptance. If a man offers me a million dollars I do not knock him down to get it. I don't have to struggle to come into possession of it. I simply take it and go home before he changes his mind! Nor do I say to him, "I am sorry but I can't take this until I can understand the intellectual basis on which it is given."

I put the money in the bank and am content to leave the intellectual basis until a later time. Now, I may never actually see the money. It may simply be placed in the bank in my name. However, if I trust the donor I go and draw checks on it and find them honored. The central experience of the Christian life is a gift which I cannot see, but which is certainly real, and mine, because I draw checks on it regularly and find them honored by God every day.

If God were unwilling to give this gift, all our striving would not make Him give it. And if He is willing to give it, there is nothing to strive for or against, except our own doubts that such a friendship is possible, and that it may be ours for the taking. With regard to "the intellectual basis" on which the gift is given, the truth is that the greatest difficulty in the matter is not intellectual at all, but the difficulty of being loyal to the Friend. And the loyalty doesn't break down through doubt, but through selfishness. We don't refuse other gifts simply because we don't understand them. Some years ago, a dear friend gave me a desktop computer. Recently, another dear friend "upgraded" the computer I presently own. I assure you that I do not understand these machines, but also assure you that I did not refuse the gifts of these friends because I do not understand the mechanics of the machine. Incidentally, I am told that they are now making a computer that is so much like a human being that when it makes a mistake, it blames another computer! I heard about a skunk that fell into a computer — and came out a stinking know-it-all! Let's see, where was I . . . Any simpleton can receive a gift. Friendship with Jesus is a gracious gift of God — and it requires a ready receiver.

The March 16, 1985, edition of *TV Guide* told the story of Lauren Tewes, an actress who was making over a million dollars a year as the co-star of the top-rated television series, Love Boat. Talent, beauty, and personality combined to make Lauren Tewes one of the most recognized people in the world. But despite the glamor that surrounded her public image, her private life became a struggle for self-worth from her first days on the set of Love Boat. Studio executives criticized her mercilessly. "I felt so insecure," she said, "I spent a lot of time trying to please people who demanded that I change myself. The public told me I was a star, but I felt like nothing."

In the attempt to escape her prison of insecurity, Lauren sought refuge in the euphoria of cocaine. But this drug eventually stole everything from her, including the last remaining shreds of her self-worth. She was fired from the series and forced to begin a long, slow struggle to rebuild her career from scratch. Only seven years after she attained television stardom, her career, her money, and her home were gone — traded for cocaine.

One morning after a sleepless night, feeling worthless and totally alone, she turned on the television and fell into bed. The screen flickered to life, and a kindly man in a red cardigan sweater smiled and said, "I'll be your friend. Will you be mine?" The parents and children of the 1960s and later will recognize the man as Fred Rogers, the host of Public Broadcasting's *Mister Rogers Neighborhood*. Fred Rogers is an ordained Presbyterian minister with the special charge to "serve children and their families through the media," and he has been gently and lovingly ministering to children on public TV for years.

When Lauren Tewes heard Mr. Rogers offer and question, "I'll be your friend. Will you be mine?" she broke down in tears and answered aloud, "Yes! Yes, I will!" She later said, "I resolved at that point to get my life together. I was totally collapsed, and Mr. Rogers saved my life — with an offer of friendship."

In much the same manner, but in a far worse sense, man was totally collapsed through sin, and facing eternal destruction. But "God was in Christ, reconciling the world unto Himself" (establishing peace and friendship between Himself and the world). Jesus died, rose again, ascended to Heaven, and sent the Holy Spirit to re-present His Case to your heart. As a part of the arrangement, He says, "I will be your Friend. Will you be Mine?" What a transformation will occur in your life if you will answer as Lauren Tewes answered Mr. Rogers, "Yes! Yes, I will!"

A Price Paid

Another dimension of this friendship is that *a high price was paid* to make it possible. We must not speak glibly about this friendship, as if it were easy and automatic. No, there was a massive barrier between God and man which prohibited such a friendship as long as the barrier stood. Man's sin stood like an impenetrable wall shutting man out from God. Sin was the breach of an Original Friendship between man and God. Sin broke that friendship (fellowship) with God. And the breach was obvious in both parties. Man became God's enemy through sin, and God became man's enemy, as well. Because of sin, men are "out of sync" with God, and become "haters of God" (Romans 1:30). And God is not passive with regard to sin; He always reacts against it. Psalm 5:4 says, "Thou are not a God that hath pleasure in wickedness; neither shall evil dwell with Thee." Indeed, "Thou hatest all workers of iniquity" (Psalm 5:5). God must hate sin because He is totally in favor of its opposite. And because every sinner is identified with his sin until he is shaken by the power of God in conversion, the reaction of God against sin determines His treatment of the sinner. God hates the perversion so much that He cannot allow it in His Holy Presence (Habakkuk 1:13) — but God still loves the person! One commentator said, "This was a problem worthy of a god, and God solved it like the God that He is." This is the very heart of the Gospel of Christ: "When we were enemies, we were reconciled to God by the death of His Son; and much more, being now reconciled, we shall be saved by His life" (Romans 5:10). "The death of His Son" — this was the price that was paid to make this transforming friendship possible.

When the Bible tells us that "the gift of God is eternal life through Jesus Christ our Lord," and that we are "saved by grace through faith, and that is not of ourselves, but it is the gift of God, not of works, lest any man should boast," we might simplify it by saying that salvation is God's gift through friendship with Jesus Christ.

THE GROWTH OF FRIENDSHIP

Second, we will consider the *growth of this transforming friendship*. One great British Christian said, "A man must keep his friendships in constant repair." This is certainly true of the greatest friendship of all. The Bible says, "A man who would have friends must show himself friendly." This simply means that if you want to draw on the bank account of personal friendship, you must make regular deposits of congeniality and relationship. The person who is a friend will always have a friend. And this is certainly true of the greatest friendship of all.

> *"One there is, above all others,*
> *Well deserves the name of Friend;*
> *His is love beyond a brother's;*
> *Costly, free, and knows no end.*
> *They who once His kindness prove*
> *Find it to be everlasting love."*

Note in the above lines that friendship must be tried, and then it will be tested and proved. Involvement and investment are big factors in a friendship. A person may "stumble into" a friendship, or "stumble upon" a new friend, but then comes the building of the relationship into a rock-ribbed friendship. This will always involve trial and error, successes and failures, laughter and tears, but a true friendship will grow stronger with every new venture.

Henry Ford once said, "Your best friend is the person who brings out the best in you." In the Presence of Jesus, men in the Gospels found a "higher, better self" emerging out of the ruins of their sinful natures. Jesus lifted men's hearts with His friendship. He saw the ideal person while looking at the real person, the potential person while looking at the actual person. But the question is, how does the real give way to the ideal? How does the potential person become the actual person?

The Law of Observation and Identification

The first "law of friendship" which we will examine could be called *the law of observation and identification*. Stated simply, this law means that you become best friends with the person you observe most closely and "hang around with" most consistently.

One of the greatest golfers in the history of the game was Bobby Jones. When Bobby Jones was a little boy, his family lived near the East Lake golf course in Atlanta, Georgia, and every afternoon after school he followed the club pro around the course, watching him play. He came to admire the golf game of this man, and he watched him ever more closely. When Bobby began to play the game of golf, his golf swing was the perfect imitation or replication of the golf swing of the club pro. It is a law of life that we become like what we live with and look at. Is it any accident that the word, "behold," occurs so many times and in so many settings in the Bible? Is it any accident that Jesus used the word so often, and it was used in addressing our attention to Him so often? I think not. Indeed, the only way this friendship can transform our lives is through observation of Jesus and identification with Him.

We can even go so far as to say that no one has ever properly "beheld" Jesus and truly identified with Him by faith without being transformed. Robert Coleman said, "No one can look very long upon Immanuel's face and remain the same," and he was right. At the end of a period of convalescence while recovering from a serious illness, the great Christian missionary E. Stanley Jones wrote, "I have spent these months looking into the face of Jesus with an unobstructed gaze, and what I see is beautiful." He was simply practicing the first law of a growing friendship, the law of observation and identification.

The Law of Association

The second "law" of friendship could be called *the law of association*. This law simply means that the friends who are most real to you are those with whom you associate most.

A young man went away from home to serve in the United States military. While he was away, he faithfully wrote a letter to his girl friend every single day. At the end of a year of receiving daily letters from him, she married the postman! That is the law of association.

When I was a teenager, I had a friend who lived next door. I saw him practically every day, and sometimes I saw him several times a day. We became almost inseparable companions. We ran around together. We fished together. We went to and from school together. We played together and worked together. I felt very close to him. The mutual influence that we had on each other was very real. But then I moved away. Because we were both poor writers, we didn't correspond with each other. After visiting back and forth a few times, we slowly lost contact. Today, we only remember each other from a far away place and a time long ago. Both the friendship and its failure are examples of the law of association. This law says that if two persons are to be real to each other, they must take time to be together.

If I wanted to practice the law of association in building a friendship, there are several practical things I might do. *First, I would spend a lot of time talking with my friend privately and personally.* One cannot spend extended periods in private conversation without opening windows of friendship. Apply this to your friendship with Jesus. How much time do you spend in secret prayer? Jesus said, "When you pray, enter into your closet, and when you have shut the door, pray to the Father who is in secret." How often do you converse with God? Someone said, "Prayer is simply holding open house for God." Thus, face to face contact is made, and a person to person association is built. In time, a friend becomes another self. In friendship with Jesus, He becomes your "other self." Aristotle spoke of a true friend as one soul in two bodies. Though the Bible says it differently, this is what union with Christ, or friendship with Jesus in its deepest sense, means.

Stanley Jones, the great missionary to India, was once visiting Copenhagen, Denmark. During his stay in Copenhagen, he visited the Church of Our Lady. While there, he viewed the famous statue created by the Danish sculptor, Thorvaldsen. He was walking silently down the aisle of the church to leave the building after viewing the statue when he was approached by a church custodian. In broken English, the man asked Dr. Jones, "Sir, did you see the Master's face?" and he gestured back to the statue. "Why, no," Jones replied, "you can't see His face; it is bowed to the ground." "Ah, but that's the point," said the custodian, "if you would see the Master's face, you must first kneel at His feet." If you would see Jesus and become best friends with Him, you must spend much time talking with Him personally.

Second, I would spend a lot of time talking with his friends. This is a second practical step to be taken in practicing the law of association. People who are friends of Jesus help us to know Him better. Jesus said, "Where two or three are gathered together in My Name, there am I in the midst of them."

In the great account of the "Emmaus Road walk" of two disciples on the evening of the resurrection of Christ, the Bible contains this enlightening verse: "And it came to pass, that, while they communed together and reasoned, Jesus Himself drew near, and went with them" (Luke 24:15). This is precisely what happens when two friends of Jesus are in proper relationship with Him, in proper relationship with each other, and are humbly discussing the things of God. "Jesus Himself draws near, and goes with them." Dear Christian, spend a lot of time in rich fellowship with the friends of Jesus talking about Him. The law of association will operate and you will know Christ better. If we would know Him better, we must develop companionship with the right kind of Christians.

Third, I would read a good book about Him. This is a third practical step to be taken in practicing the law of association. Even so, if I want to know Jesus better, I must make much of His Book. God's best gift to the world is His Son. His second best gift to the world is the Bible. No one can ignore the Bible and improve his friendship with Jesus.

If I wanted to know George Washington better, what might I do? I would go to the local library in my community and get a book about him and sit down and read it. In fact, I know many of the great characters of history far better than I know many of my own neighbors — because of the law of association. I have read good books about many people from the past, and though I have never seen any of them, I have gotten to "know" them quite well. Never underestimate the power of a good book if you want to get to know someone better.

Henry Ward Beecher wrote, "I never knew my mother. She died when I was only four years of age. But one day I was reading over a lot of letters that my mother wrote to my father, and I found the letters that she wrote from the day they met until their love was one. When I read these letters, I think I understood my mother." You and I have never seen Jesus in the flesh, but we have an incredible volume of "letters" which expose His heart to us.

Gutson Borglum, the great sculptor, wrote about his technique in these words: "I studied every known photograph of the subject. I read every book about him I could find. I looked up many who had seen him, and talked with them. Then I had my own mental picture and reproduced it." Here again is the law of association.

Pastor Charles E. Jefferson said, "I feel as though I know Paul better than any man who ever lived. I made Paul my daily companion. I read his letters over and over again. I read everything I could find which has been written about Paul; I have thought about him, and talked about him, so now I feel as if I know Paul better than I know any other man who ever lived."

George W. Truett, perhaps the greatest statesman ever to emerge from Baptist ranks, said, "If men are rooted and grounded in a knowledge of the Bible, they will go out against any sin, against any foe, against any difficulty, and they will overcome, for the Bible is a signboard pointing us to Christ."

How much time did you spend yesterday with the world and its affairs by means of your newspaper or television? And how much, by comparison, did you spend with God in the pages of His Book?

This is the law of association. If you want to know Jesus better, talk with Him privately and personally, talk with His friends, and read a good book about Him. These are practical ways to use the law of association.

The Law of Expression

There is a third law of friendship which is as fundamental as the others. It could be called *the law of expression*. This law means that friendship feeds on any outward expression that is given to it. If I express myself positively and practically toward another person, I get to know that person better by means of that expression. Let me suggest some practical ways to improve a friendship by means of the law of expression.

First, follow the friend. This is the practical side of the law of identification which I mentioned earlier. Identify with the friend in consistent association and activity. Over and over, Jesus said, "Follow me." No one can hope to be the friend of Jesus if he does not heed this admonition and take advantage of this invitation. Jesus said, "I am the light of the world. He who follows after Me shall not walk in darkness, but shall have the light of life." In John 10:27, He supplied two "tests of friendship" when He said, "My sheep hear my voice, and I know them, and they follow me." You improve your friendship with any person when you follow him.

Second, express yourself in some act of practical service. Genuine friendship thrives on deeds more than words. You can express your friendship in words, and you ought to, but the words will become hollow unless sometimes you let your actions speak as well as your words. The gift you sent on Mother's Day has drawn you closer to your mother. The cake you baked for your neighbor who was entertaining guests has strengthened the neighborly association. The food you fixed and sent to your sick friend, the visit you paid to the hospital, the note of encouragement you sent to the distant friend — these expressions of friendship have brought you closer to your friend. Christian, how long has it been since you went out of your way to do something for God?

I Corinthians 3:9 says that "we are laborers together with God." However, it is obvious that laborers labor. It is astounding to see how many Christians only read the Bible occasionally, pray occasionally, go to church (occasionally!), and then wonder why their relationship with Christ is not more real and vital. The abiding life of John 15 is an active life; the more aggressive the action, the more vital the life.

Daniel 11:31 gives us an acid test of this friendship. It says, "The people who know their God shall be strong, and shall do great exploits." Aggressive practical service for your friend is one of the great tests of genuine friendship.

The idle Christian is always in trouble spiritually. Idleness explains a thousand doubts and a thousand defeats. Even John the Baptist, the bold prophet who uncompromisingly called wicked King Herod to repent of his sin, when he was put in jail, and had a period of enforced inactivity, fell into doubt and depression through idleness (Matthew 11:2-3). Let your love for Christ begin to speak the language of deeds and you will soon have an enlarged relationship with Him.

Third, talk about your friend to someone else. Tell somebody what you think of him, and your relationship with him will grow. We are so constructed as human beings that no thought, no feeling, no impulse is fully ours until we have expressed it. And the more frequent the expression, the more complete the possession. This can be tested in any relationship. Just speak of your love to your parents or your children, and that love becomes more real. Tell somebody what you think of Jesus. Tell them how much you love Him. Describe Him to them, and your love for Him will grow.

These, then, are the "laws" by which friendship operates and grows. If they are practiced in your friendship with Jesus, it will be kept in good repair, and will grow.

THE GAIN OF FRIENDSHIP

When Elizabeth Barrett Browning was asked the secret of her life, she simply replied, "I had a friend." Anyone who knows Mrs. Browning's story can well guess that she was referring to her relationship with her loving husband, Robert, who was instrumental in bringing Elizabeth out of a tragic home background and instilling in her self-worth that enabled her to become what she likely would never have been otherwise. Whatever Mrs. Browning meant by her testimony, any genuine Christian would happily give the same testimony as the "secret" of his life. "I had a Friend!" No greater gain in life can be had than the gain that comes through a personal friendship with the glorious Son of God.

History records that Sir Philip Sidney, poet, philosopher, and soldier of the sixteenth century, fell in battle on the field of Zutphen in the year 1586. In his great distress he called for a drink of water; but as he was putting the cup to his lips, he saw near him another dying man whose eyes were fixed longingly on the cup. Lowering his hand, Sidney handed him the cup, declaring weakly, "Your necessity is greater than mine." Many acts like that made his name famous for kindness and grace. So it was not strange that a knight of that time requested that this epitaph be put above his grave: "Here lies the friend of Sir Philip Sidney." Any sensitive and genuine Christian might want these words on his tombstone: "Here lies the friend of Jesus Christ. I was one who was befriended by Him, and transformed by the friendship!"

What have I gained by this friendship? What power has come to me through it?

The Power of Example

A Christian's friendship with Jesus brings into his life an incredible *power of example*. No one will ever be able to testify that Jesus Christ set a bad example for Him to follow! Though Jesus has given me infinitely more than a good example, it is certainly true that He has "left me an example, that I should follow His steps" (I Peter 2:22).

The Power of Experience

Any friendship will inevitably mean *the transfer of some power, some influence, some experience*. The two friends will tend to become like one another, and both will be stronger than before. This will occur whether the strength be that of evil or of good. One nature feeds on another, and the nourishment received is the greatest in a true friendship. Normally, the weaker of the two feeds on the stronger, so that the weaker becomes stronger through the communication of personality that occurs in the friendship.

You might think of the two friends as two highly charged electric terminals, and the "spark" of power passes from the higher to the lower, or from the positive to the negative. Many people are "attracted" to Jesus Christ; many people "admire" Him. But this attraction, this admiration, bring no real gain to an individual's life. In fact, it is likely that no human being can help being attracted to Jesus when He really sees Him. But true power flows only through a solid friendship with Him.

One of the great experiences that comes through this friendship is *the experience of consolidation*. A believer's friendship with Jesus will run through every part of his life just as a thread runs through a necklace of beads and unites them. That thread will give to even the smallest bead an important place, a significant meaning, and a great value. Even so, this transforming friendship will focus a life into a unit and rescue it from division and waste. To follow the analogy negatively, without this friendship, the experiences of life are scattered as loose beads on a living room floor. But this friendship is like the thread that gathers up all the loose beads and makes them all part of one great whole. This friendship gives meaning and blessing to every experience of life.

Another of the great blessings of this friendship is *its duration.* A verse in Proverbs says that "a friend loves at all times, and a brother is born for adversity." Some people make "fair-weather friends," the kind who are not "born for adversity." Adversity is often the wind that separates the chaff of flattery from the grain of real friendship.

The Shadow once said to the Body: "Who is a friend like me? I follow you wherever you go. In sunlight or in moonlight I never forsake you." "True," replied the Body. "You go with me in sunlight and in moonlight. But where are you when neither sun nor moon shines upon me?" The friendship of Jesus does not rise and fall like the tide. It is not probated on our performance. It endures through all circumstances and threats.

The Power of Expulsion

One of the greatest gains of this transforming friendship with Jesus is *the power of expulsion* which it brings into the Christian's life. When this friendship has been firmly established, a lot of lesser issues are automatically settled. A lot of questions are answered, a lot of temptations are overcome, a lot of problems are resolved — by this friendship. This friendship throws the entire bias of the believer's life into an elevated course, and prevents him from wasting himself on a lower one.

> "In sin I long had found delight,
> Unawed by shame and fear,
> Till a new object struck my sight,
> And stopped my wild career."

One of the most popular hymns ever written is entitled, "What a Friend We Have In Jesus." I am quite happy and comfortable when singing it. Jesus Christ has proven His friendship to me again and again. However, it occurs to me that we are usually singing of a one-sided relationship. We are singing of His friendship with us, but not necessarily of our friendship with Him. I found that when I turned the words around and tried to sing, "What a friend I am to Jesus," I was hardly comfortable at all. I felt that the acclamation of the first title had become an accusation if I turned the words around. Then I read in the Book of James that "Abraham was called the friend of God," and my appreciation for Abraham immediately grew. What could be more glorious than to be a friend of God? A friend of Jesus? Remember, I am a friend of Jesus only because I have been befriended by Him, but how balanced is the friendship?

Most parents can remember a time when one of their children, when small, brought into the house some neighborhood child (and it might have been an urchin or a derelict) and announced proudly, "This is my friend." I'm sure that Jesus makes such a presentation of me — and will reaffirm it One Day in Heaven — but the question lingers, How good a friend am I to Him? Is anyone in your community able to say about you, "That person is a friend of Jesus"?

Many years ago, a great little Scottish book was published, entitled, *Men of the Knotted Heart*. It is the story of outstanding Christian Scotsmen who were bound together by a common hot-hearted relationship with Jesus Christ. The truly fascinating thing about it is that the title is the Hebrew idiom for "friendship." Christian, is your heart intertwined, knotted, with the heart of Jesus? If so, then you are His friend.

We have a denomination in Christendom who are called "Friends." I am not willing to relinquish or concede the title to them. I want to be a friend — a best friend — of Jesus.

Chapter 16

The Divine Drama of Salvation

"Not as though I had already attained, either were already perfect: but I follow after, if that I may apprehend that for which also I was apprehended of Christ Jesus. Brethren, I count not myself to have apprehended; but this one thing I do, forgetting those things which are behind, and reaching forth unto those things which are before, I press toward the mark for the prize of the high calling of God in Christ Jesus" (Philippians 3:12-14).

The most important thing about a lost man is that he is a sinner in character and dead in condition. In himself, he is a sinner, and in his relationship with God, he is dead. A lost man functions out of only two-thirds of his being (body and soul); he is "not all here" (his spirit is dead). So the all-determinative, all-important part of his nature, his spirit, is totally dead in the only relationship that matters, his relationship with God. Furthermore, a great miracle is required to let the lost man know that he is in this condition. So *two miracles are required* for a lost man to be brought into right relationship with God — the *miracle of conviction* (which causes him to know that he is lost), and the *miracle of conversion* (by which he is introduced to God).

The New Testament uses six big words to describe Divine salvation. One is *justification*. In justification, the sinner is guilty before a just and holy God, and God graciously declares him not guilty through his faith in Jesus Christ.

A second word is *redemption*. In redemption, the sinner is seen as a slave, and is bought out of the slave market by the precious blood of Christ, and set free.

A third word is *regeneration*. In regeneration, the sinner is dead, and God, in his grace, infuses him with Divine, spiritual, eternal life.

A fourth word is *adoption*. In adoption, the sinner is an alien, estranged from God, and God graciously places him in status before Him as a full-grown, mature son.

A fifth word is *reconciliation*. In reconciliation, the sinner is an enemy of God, not only out of relationship but in revolt against God, and God graciously removes the cause of the enmity and brings the sinner into a standing and condition of peace with God.

A sixth word is *conversion*. In conversion, the sinner is a fleeing fugitive, and God stops him in his flight and turns him around, turning Him forever toward Himself.

This sixth word, conversion, is the word that is highlighted in our text. And it is the most dramatic side of conversion that is revealed here. Verse ten tells us that the Christian life is a matter of "knowing Christ." That is, it is a matter of regular, intimate personal relationship between me and Jesus. Verse twelve tells us how this relationship was established, how it began. The King James Bible says, "I was apprehended of Christ Jesus." The key word is "apprehended." Other translations say, "I was laid hold of by Christ Jesus." The word is a highly dramatic word. It means "to arrest" or "to capture." One translation daringly says, "Christ Jesus put a stranglehold on me." It is a law officer's word, a word that would be used for a person apprehended by the law enforcement officers of a community.

Note the title that is given to the Arresting Officer. "I was arrested by Christ Jesus." This title provides one of the great themes of the book of Philippians. The name always follows this order, "Christ Jesus." The order we usually follow is "Jesus Christ," but Paul's order is usually "Christ Jesus." "Jesus" is His human name. One commentator called it "the Christmas Name of God." "Christ" is one of His Divine titles, the title which reveals His Heavenly appointment and anointment in coming to the earth. So the order of these names, "Christ Jesus," reveals a downward direction, from heaven to earth. This is the direction the Arresting Officer followed in coming to arrest sinners. You see, sinners seek God in the same manner in which a mouse seeks a cat — not at all! And, as with the mouse and cat, the reason for the sinner's flight from God is fear. Romans 3:11 says, "There is none who understands, there is none who seeks after God." If God and sinners are ever to be reconciled, an Arresting Officer must come from Heaven, arrest the sinner, and press His claims for peace and restored relationship. And, glory to God, that is precisely what the text tells us has happened!

"I stand as one who has been arrested," Paul says. The verb is an aorist passive indicative. Grammatically, the indicative indicates real action. So this word describes a real-life occurrence; it is not merely a figure of speech. The passive voice of the verb means that someone else did the arresting; sinners don't merely "turn themselves in" to the arresting officer. And the aorist tense means that the "arrest" occurred only once! However, the results continue indefinitely.

Paul pursued the same kind of analogy in II Corinthians 2:14-16 when he said, "Thanks be to God, who always leads us in His triumph in Christ." This is the picture of a conquering war hero, who brings his prisoners back home chained to his chariot and being pulled by him at his pace wherever He wants to take them. *The conqueror is Christ, the "prisoners" are all believers, and the triumphal procession is the Christian life.* The words, "arrested" and "led in triumph" are sovereign, powerful words. And how realistic they are! When Jesus Christ saves you, He wants you to "ride up on the driver's seat with Him," but it is obvious that there is a strong, subtle factor within you -- the "flesh" -- which makes that impossible. There is no joint Lordship! Yet He loves you too much to abandon you and cast you off. So He chains you to His chariot wheels! This truth is echoed in the conversion testimony of the great Oxford scholar, C. S. Lewis. He said, "That night, I was dragged kicking and screaming into the Kingdom of God, probably the most reluctant convert in the history of Christendom." The Christian has been arrested and imprisoned by the grace of God, and he is never to forget this relationship.

In this study, we will explore the meaning of this word, "arrested," in order to better understand the nature of our relationship with Jesus Christ.

SERIOUS CRIMES

First, the powerful word, "arrested," suggests that some serious crimes have been committed. Normally, it is a criminal that is arrested. So this word brings us to abruptly face the horrible truth about man, the truth of his sins, his crimes against God and His Law.

A crime has been committed — by man, and against God. The Bible calls this crime "sin." In a very real sense, Christianity begins with sin. And so did your life (Psalm 51:5). The coming of Jesus Christ into the world had to do with the sins of humanity. You see, as far as we know, God has never had but one problem in His Eternal History, and that is the problem of sin. Man is charged before the High Court of the universe with multiple crimes, and not one of them is a mere misdemeanor. In fact, each crime is so serious that it deserves eternity in the Prison House of the universe. What are the crimes? What are your crimes?

First, you have flagrantly stolen your entire life from God's hand. So sin is a stewardship violation which involves embezzlement and grand larceny. *And the crime was committed against God, and in favor of Satan.*

God made every human being, and thus He has first claim on each person's life. "It is He who has made us, and not we ourselves."

Then, God daily sustains each person. "It is in Him that we live, and move, and have our being, and our very breath is in His hand." Every breath that human beings breathe is sponsored by God. In Jesus' well-known story of the prodigal son, when the boy departed from his home and went into a far country, Jesus said that he "wasted his resources in riotous living." Whose resources? The very resources the father had given him! Sin is the prostitution of Divine resources which have been given to men to manage and improve. And, wonder of wonders, God "sponsors the sin" by providing the resources by which the sin is committed. He gives the tongue to the cursing blasphemer. He gives the feet to the straying sinner. He gives the brain to the plotting rebel. He sponsors your life, even when you live in sin!

Then God bought you — at an incredibly high price. A United States astronaut was widely interviewed by representatives of the news media after he returned from walking on the moon. One reporter asked, "What were your thoughts when you stood on the moon and looked back toward the earth?" The astronaut facetiously replied, "I remembered that I was to return to earth on a space vehicle that had been built by the lowest bidder!" God never tried to get by with the lowest bid. He purchased sinners (worthless sinners) at full price, a price of His choosing.

Years ago, a Norwegian pastor named Josef Nordenhaug was president of the Baptist World Alliance. During his presidency, the Alliance met in convention in London, England. Nordenhaug and his wife were staying in a hotel in London, along with several of his ministerial friends. One morning, he had left his wife, slightly ill, with another pastor's wife in their hotel room and had gone with his fellow pastor to eat breakfast. They went to a restaurant just a short distance from the hotel. On their return walk to the hotel, a prostitute approached them and propositioned them. After listening to her invitation, Dr. Nordenhaug said, "Come with us, please."

And the two men led her into their hotel and took her up to his room. When they entered the room, Dr. Nordenhaug asked, "What was the price?" When she answered, he said, "Young lady, do you know that you are selling yourself far too cheaply? You are worth much more than that. I want to introduce you to a friend of mine, who can tell you how much you are really worth." He then took the woman into his wife's bedroom, where the two preacher's wives led the young woman to Christ.

Sin means that I disregard my creation by God, God's daily sustaining of my life, and Christ's great purchase of me at Calvary. Sin is "autonomy," or the practice of "self-law." It means that I withhold myself from God and set my own standards for my life. The Bible says (Romans 3:22-23), "There is no difference, for all have sinned and come short of the glory of God." The word translated "sin" in that verse means "to miss the mark." As a human being, the character target I am to "shoot for" is the character (or the "glory") of God.

Several years ago, the San Francisco Giants were in the post-season divisional playoffs to determine which teams would play in the baseball World Series. During one of the playoff games, a parachutist dramatically descended through the skies, attempting to land at home plate inside the stadium. However, due to a miscalculation of wind currents which regularly swirl at Candlestick Park in San Francisco, the chutist missed the stadium altogether. Even so, all men have missed the assigned mark of God's character. They have "fallen short of the glory of God." Instead of hitting the mark of God's character, they have become self-addicted. So sin means to be under-related to God and over-related to self. And this over-relation to self has caused you to practice "theomania," which is your crazy attempt to play the role of God for yourself.

Sin is man's "God-Almightiness," that lifestyle by which a man curls his entire life right back on himself. Someone insightfully defined sin as "man's private purposing." Sin (S-I-N) is Self-Ish-Ness. Note the "big I," the perpendicular pronoun, in the middle of the word, "sIn." The same letter is in the middle of the words "prIde" and "LucIfer." Sin is the character condition of having the "big I" at the control center of your life. To be a sinner means that you have chosen to be "marooned on an 'I-land' called Self." And this means that you have stolen and embezzled your life from God's hand. As a kind of spiritual "self-napping," this is a criminal act of major proportions.

But the sinner's crimes are worse even than theft or embezzlement. Every sin is a God-killer! Sin is a slap in God's face and a stab into God's heart. So the slightest sin in your life implicates you in a charge of murder. In *Thus Spake Zarathustra,* Friedrich Nietzsche identifies man as "the murderer of God." He was right! This is the meaning of the Cross of Christ. When God was human on earth, man murdered Him on a cross. When man got his hands on God, God's violent death was the outcome.

The Cross of Christ was a timeless thing. It stands as an Eternal Deed (Revelation 13:8). It is as if it were reconstructed or reenacted every day. Just as the nails of the cross rendered Jesus inactive and dead, so your sins render Him inactive and dead. Just as the nail in His hand incapacitated the serving hand of Jesus, so your sins incapacitate Him and His serving hand. Sin is a grievous act of murder — committed against God!

The artist Rembrandt, in his renowned painting of the crucifixion of Christ, painted his own face on the body of one of the crucifying soldiers. It was his way of confessing his own implication in the Death of the Son of God. Dear friend, there is a live trail of blood between you and Calvary! There is a fresh blood-trail between me and the Cross. If I remain lost, that blood-trail will mean my eternal condemnation in Hell. If I am saved, that blood-trail reminds me of my cleansing by the blood of Christ (I John 1:7). Philippians 3:18 says that "many walk ... who are the enemies of the Cross of Christ, whose end is destruction." This means that, without Christ, you are the decided enemy of your only hope. By your sins, you have murdered the Son of God. And this attempted Deicide is actually suicide. In your attempt to kill God, your only final target is yourself!

Aurelius Augustine, one of the greatest of theologians, said, "My sin was all the more incredible because I did not think myself to be a sinner." Sin, which often appears to be "innocent" or insignificant to the perpetrator, is actually a combination of the greatest of crimes against God, the crimes of theft and murder. And these crimes are infinitely serious. The seriousness of any crime is partially determined by the nature and significance of the person or thing against which it is committed. After David had committed adultery with Bathsheba and had murdered her husband, Uriah, he nonetheless said to God, "Against Thee, and Thee only have I sinned, and done this evil in Thy sight" (Psalm 51:4). By its very nature, all sin is a heinous act committed against God. The word "arrested" suggests that some serious crimes have been committed, and indeed they have.

A SAD COURSE

Second, the word "arrested" suggests that *a sad course* has been taken by the guilty criminal. Whereas he should have "given himself up" and "thrown himself on the mercy of the court," he has further misrepresented God and compounded his own guilt by fleeing from God, from justice, and from mercy. Instead of running to God, he acts like a guilty and condemned criminal and runs from God. Thus, he becomes a refugee from God and from grace.

In one of the greatest poems ever written, Francis Thompson pictures man's flight and his plight in stanza after stanza. The title of the poem is "The Hound of Heaven." It is an incredibly insightful admission of both guilt and hope in a fleeing sinner. Here are some of its words.

> "I fled Him, down the nights and down the days;
> I fled Him, down the arches of the years;
> I fled Him, down the puzzling hallways
> Of my own mind, and in the mist of tears
> I hid from Him, and under running laughter.
> Up vistaed hopes, I sped; And shot, precipitated,
> Adown Titanic glooms of chasmed fears,

> *From those strong Feet that followed, followed after.*
> *But with unhurrying chase, And unperturbed pace,*
> *Deliberate speed, majestic instancy,*
> *They beat — and a Voice beat,*
> *More instant than the Feet:*
> *'All things betray thee, who betrayest Me.'*

Listen to the conclusions of each of the long stanzas:
> "*Nigh and nigh draws the chase,*
> *With unperturbed pace,*
> *Deliberate speed, majestic instancy,*
> *And past those noised Feet*
> *A Voice comes yet more fleet --*
> *'Lo! Naught contents thee, who content'st not Me.'*
> "*Halts by me that footfall:*
> *Is my gloom after all,*
> *Shade of His hand, outstretched caressingly? —*
> *Ah, fondest, blindest, weakest,*
> *I am He Whom thou seekest!*
> *Thou drovest love from thee, who drovest Me.'*

You have just read some remarkably vivid lines of Divine-human dialogue, in which the sinner is being brought to realize the nature and seriousness of his flight from God. Today, millions need to see themselves as guilty parties in a massive revolt against Heaven and Heaven's God, an insurrection of vast proportions. This is the sad course that sinners take by fleeing from God.

A SPIRITUAL CRISIS

Third, this text suggests the spiritual crisis that is necessary in the sinner's life if he is ever to come to his proper destiny. "I have been arrested," Paul said. A capture has occurred!

Turn again to Acts chapter nine and read the story of Paul's conversion (Acts 9:1-18). Note that the "arrester" was himself "arrested"! Let me read the story from a live paraphrase of the New Testament, *The Message,* translated by Eugene Peterson.

"All this time Paul was breathing down the necks of the Master's disciples, out for the kill. He went to the Chief Priest and got arrest warrants to take to the meeting places in Damascus so that if he found anyone there belonging to the Way, whether men or women, he could arrest them and bring them to Jerusalem.

He set off. When he got to the outskirts of Damascus, he was suddenly dazed by a blinding flash of light. As he fell to the ground, he heard a voice: 'Saul, Saul, why are you out to get me?' He said, 'Who are you, Master?' 'I am Jesus, the One you're hunting down. I want you to get up and enter the city. In the city you'll be told what to do next.'

His companions stood there dumbstruck — they could hear the sound, but couldn't see anyone — while Saul, picking himself up off the ground, found himself stone blind. They had to take him by the hand and lead him into Damascus. He continued blind for three days. He ate nothing, drank nothing.

There was a disciple in Damascus by the name of Ananias. The Master spoke to him in a vision: 'Ananias.' 'Yes, Master?' he answered. 'Get up and go over to Straight Avenue. Ask at the house of Judas for a man from Tarsus. His name is Saul. He's there praying. He has just had a dream in which he saw a man named Ananias enter the house and lay hands on him so he could see again.'

Ananias protested, 'Master, you can't be serious. Everybody's talking about this man and the terrible things he's been doing, his reign of terror against your people in Jerusalem! And now he's shown up here with papers from the Chief Priest that give him license to do the same to us."

But the Master said, 'Don't argue. Go! I have picked him as my personal representative to Gentiles and kings and Jews. And now I'm about to show him what he's in for — the hard suffering that goes with this job.'

So Ananias went and found the house, placed his hands on blind Saul, and said, 'Brother Saul, the Master sent me, the same Jesus you saw on your way here. He sent me so you could see again and be filled with the Holy Spirit.' No sooner were the words out of his mouth than something *like scales fell from Saul's eyes — he could see again! He got to his feet, was baptized, and sat down with them to a hearty meal."*

This vivid account helps to explain the word "arrest" as a salvation word. "Suddenly there shone a light." You see, God must turn His Light on in you and on you before you can be saved. And never does your fugitive flight from Him show up so clearly as here. "This is the condemnation, that light has come into the world, and men loved darkness rather than light, because their deeds were evil. For every one that doeth evil hateth the light, neither cometh to the light, lest his deeds should be reproved. But he that doeth truth cometh to the light, that his deeds may be made manifest, that they are wrought in God" (John 3:19-21). So Paul's conversion was a *specimen case*, a case which illustrates and dramatizes the nature of all conversion. In fact, in I Timothy 1:16, Paul wrote, "I obtained mercy, that in me first Jesus Christ might show forth all long-suffering, for a pattern to them which should hereafter believe on Him to life everlasting."

Picture a police helicopter circling near a crime-scene at night, seeking a fugitive. A bright light is streaming down from the search vehicle, sweeping the ground beneath. Suddenly that circle of light falls upon the fugitive criminal, discovering and isolating him for the arrest. This is a true picture of what happens when a person is saved.

We have often heard of "the long arm of the law." Not long ago, I read Victor Hugo's great novel, *Les Miserables*. Throughout the book, the relentless law is seen pursuing a "guilty" criminal, Jean Valjean. But the book is gloriously overshadowed by another long arm and stretched-out hand, the arm of God's redeeming love. Victor Hugo, a Christian, used his great novel as a vehicle of faith in the overcoming power of God's saving love, and the book is a great monument to that faith. In the "arrest" of a sinner by God's power and grace, both of these arms — the long arms of Divine Law and Divine Love — reach the sinner and arrest him. The Law prosecutes the purpose of the Holy Justice of God, and Love performs the purposes which are necessary to save man. And both are satisfied in the Cross of Christ. There, justice is exhausted and mercy is extended. There -- at the Cross -- "mercy and truth have met together, and righteousness and peace have kissed each other" (Psalm 85:10). Hallelujah!

Every sinner should see himself standing before the August Throne of the Holy God of the universe. He should see himself brokenly declaring, "If it please the Court, I have come to confess a crime." He should hear The Voice saying to him, "You are the criminal?" "Yes, I am." "And what is the nature of the crime to which you are pleading guilty?" "Oh, God....OH, GOD! I am guilty of Grand Theft — and MURDER!!!! I place myself at the mercy of this Court."

Now, bring a glorious text of God's Law Book to mind. "Thou, Lord, art good, and ready to forgive, and plenteous in mercy unto all that call upon Thee" (Psalm 86:5). Though I am perfectly and totally condemned by the Law, God has found a way to satisfy the demands of the Law and pardon and justify me! But before I would ever appreciate all the dimensions of this Gospel, there had to be a Grand Arrest. Yes, I have been arrested — and I will be eternally grateful for it!

Some years ago, the national newspapers carried the amazing story of a fourteen-year-old boy who worked in the city zoo in Chicago, Illinois. Quite apparently, he had a great love for animals, and could express that love in the environment of the city zoo. One day, several deadly gaboon vipers were brought to the zoo in a tight case. They were in the office, waiting to be defanged and put on display in the reptile section of the zoo. The young boy slipped into the office, opened the case that contained them, and carried them out onto the streets in a burlap sack! Down the street he went, with the sack slung loosely over his shoulder! One wrong move, and he would have been dead in a few minutes! He boarded a city bus, and placed the sack on the seat beside him. Meanwhile, the zoo officials had discovered the theft, guessed the identity of the criminal, and called the police with the information. The police acted quickly, enclosing a large area of the city of Chicago with their search, hoping to arrest the boy before the deadly snakes had done their natural work. Picture the scene when they finally "apprehended" him. He thought they were only apprehending him to prosecute him for his crime, but in reality, they were trying to save his life! Even so, sinners flee from God, seeing him only as a prosecuting Judge (like Jauvier in *Les Miserables*), when in reality, He is the only one who can save their lives!

If we were to apply the illustration, we would need to make this adjustment. Dear sinner, you have already been bitten by "that old serpent, the Devil"! One effect of the venomous poison is to cloud your vision so that you can only see God as a Prosecutor, when in reality He in interested in prevention and rescue. To use Francis Thompson's analogy, the "Hound of Heaven" is breathing hard on your trail. To follow Paul's figure, the Lord High Sheriff of the universe is closing in on you, and He is about to throw the "cuffs of grace" around "the wrists of your soul" and "drag you off to the cell of salvation and service," from which you will never escape — nor will you want to!

Years ago, there lived a Presbyterian preacher named Todd Hall. Todd Hall's conversion is a remarkable illustration of the Divine Arrest of sinners. Mr. Hall was by vocation a detective. One day, when D. L. Moody, the great evangelist, was conducting meetings in Baltimore, Todd Hall was on the trail of a "Most Wanted" criminal in Baltimore, trying to arrest him. The trail led him to downtown Baltimore. He was closing in on the suspect, and it appeared that he was ready to make the arrest. The criminal, knowing that he was pursued, was looking for an escape route or a place to hide. He ducked into a public building. It "just happened" that it was a meeting hall, and it "just happened" that it was a particular evening of Mr. Moody's evangelistic campaign there. The fugitive saw the crowd as a possible hiding place, so he slipped inside and quickly made his way into the audience, finding an empty seat down near the front on one side of the auditorium. From this vantage point, he could watch the door for the approach of his pursuer. Mr. Hall came in, spotted his subject, and paused a moment to plot the arrest in a manner which would least disturb the audience. While he waited, the power of Mr. Moody's message began to give him pause. He found himself "disarmed" by the great Gospel which Mr. Moody was preaching. Soon, he had all but forgotten the reason for his entrance into the hall. Remaining throughout the message, when the invitation was given, the FBI officer abandoned his 'hunt" and went forward to give his heart to Jesus Christ. The "hunter" had become the "hunted"! The arresting officer had become the arrested one! The small hunt was completely forgotten in favor of Heaven's Big Hunt. Mr. Hall left the detective service, joined Heaven's "Lost and Found Bureau," and became part of God's Arresting Force.

Joy Davidman (who became the wife of C. S. Lewis) wrote, "Every Christian conversion is the story of a blessed defeat." The greatest and happiest day in the life of any human being is when Jesus Christ arrests him and holds conquest over his soul. Lord, I thank you that you didn't honor my selfish desire and let me escape. Instead, you captured me, and you are now in the process of conquering me. What amazing grace! George Matheson, the great blind preacher, captured the "capture" in these great lines:

> "Make me a captive, Lord, and I shall be free
> Force me to render up my sword,
> And I shall conqueror be;
> I sink in life's alarms when by myself I stand;
> Imprison me within Thine arms,
> And strong shall be my hand."

Chapter 17

Wanted: Men who will Follow the Model

"Brethren, be followers together of me, and mark them which walk so as ye have us for an ensample" (Philippians 3:17; King James Version).

"Brethren, together follow my example and observe those who live after the pattern we have set you" (Philippians 3:17; Amplified Bible translation).

This text might immediately throw a shallow Christian into protest. He might say, "Who but an egotist would say, 'Brethren, join in imitating me'?" However, this assessment overlooks several very important facts from the life of the Apostle Paul, as well as several important facts revealed in the context of this verse.

Fact Number One: the moral confusion of the world of Paul's day is known to have been very great. *People needed moral and spiritual examples that could be trusted.* Paul did not back down from this duty, and he encouraged other believers to also assume the responsibility of Christian example.

Fact Number Two: the context of this verse needs to be examined carefully, because *it corrects the possibility of a charge of egotism against the one who wrote these words.* Paul has just stated in no uncertain terms that he was not perfect. "I have not already reached the goal of the Christian life, nor have I become perfect, but I press on in order that I may lay hold of that for which also I was laid hold of by Christ Jesus" (verse 12). In fact, Paul clearly indicates that the only worthy example of a Christian is the person who admits he is not perfect but is nonetheless pressing on. He has just said that he personally has no righteousness of his own; any righteousness he has is provided by Another (verse 9). Thus, the only righteousness others are to respect in Paul is the very righteousness of Christ Himself.

Then, look just beyond our text (verse 17), and read verses 18 and 19: "For many walk, of whom I have told you often, and tell you now in tears, that they are the enemies of the cross of Christ, whose end is destruction, whose god is their belly, whose glory is in their shame, who mind earthly things." After reading those words, it becomes quite obvious why Paul wrote what he did in verse 17. There were plenty of bad examples to observe, but all men (including Christians) need good examples.

Fact Number Three: in this verse, Paul called on the Philippian Christians *to imitate* not only him, but also other exemplary Christians. Hear the words again: "Brethren, be followers together of me, and mark them which walk so as ye have us for an example." The New American Standard Version says, "And observe those who walk according to the pattern you have in us." So Paul guards both himself and his disciples in this statement. He guards himself against the pride of thinking that he is the only exemplary Christian on the premises, and he guards them against following him exclusively, which might tend to create a cult. Nevertheless, Paul lovingly and boldly asks them to imitate and follow him.

THE PRACTICAL METHOD OF MAKING DISCIPLES

Just as it did with Jesus, disciple-making begins with a *model*, a *mandate*, and a *method*. The model provides the incarnational example of the process. The mandate clearly shows the responsibility of each Christian. The method combines the model and the mandate in a practical procedure, and reveals their ongoing impact.

The model is in personal example

Christian, the truth is that people will either take you as *an example of Christ,* or as *an exemption from Christ.* You cannot escape the exerting of influence, the setting of example. D. L. Moody was probably correct when he said, "Of one hundred men, one will read the Bible, and the other ninety-nine will read the Christian." You see, everything we say is a profession of faith, and everything we do is a promotion of faith. It is either an encouragement in favor of good, or of less good, or of evil. We daily influence our intimates and the immediate circle of associates just beyond them, whether we are conscious of our influence or not. A stone thrown into a pond does not merely disturb the water in the spot where it hits it. Around that point of impact, great concentric circles form. We simply cannot control our influence, though we certainly can largely control the kind of influence we exert.

> *"I have a little shadow,*
> *That goes in and out with me;*
> *And what can be the use of him,*
> *Is often more than I can see."*

Behind these ideas rests a gigantic law of spiritual life, and it is this: Christianity is propositional, to be sure, but its first attraction to human beings is generally personal. It is instructional, but it is first incarnational. Historian Robert Wilken said it wisely when he said, "Before people are doers, they are first spectators." Christianity is not merely audible, it is also visual and tangible (see I John 1:1-3). So it must have models; it must have pacesetters; it must have examples. This is one of the roles Jesus plays for mankind — "leaving us an example, to follow in His steps" (I Peter 2:21).

This is a key role, also, for every disciple-maker. He cannot expect his disciples to be what he is not, or to do what he does not do, or to go where he does not go. It is true that the disciple-maker's life must not be the end of the disciple's quest, but merely the example of one seeking to be a follower of Christ. But *it is example that gives credibility to leadership*. Jesus exemplified the standard of disciple-making before He exhorted it.

Reconsider for a moment the characteristics of a disciple. A disciple is one who: (1) has a *regular relationship* with his disciple-maker, his teacher (compare Mark 3:14a); (2) *receives revelation* from his disciple-maker, his teacher (see Matthew 10:5); (3) *shows increasing resemblance* to his disciple-maker, his teacher (see Luke 6:40); and (4) *becomes a reflection* of his teacher in both concept and conduct. So a disciple-maker must be a model and a pace-setter, and he must expect his disciples to follow him and his example. Indeed, he must humbly invite them to do so, as Paul does in our text.

The mandate is in personal exhortation

Let's examine this verse more closely, in order to be sure that we understand the dimensions of responsibility that are presented here. Indeed, we must recognize that the responsibility is two-fold. Paul had to show it and say it, and the Philippian readers had to see it and submit to it. The two key verbs, "join in following my example," and "observe those who so walk," are both in the present tense. Again, we must note that Paul boldly urged Christians to follow the example of the testimony and technique of other Christians. This means that the following of right examples should be the consistent and continuous activity of every Christian. It also suggests that most Christians need to be encouraged by another Christian to do this, or the concept will lapse in their minds.

Pastor Rick Yohn, in his book, *Living Securely In an Unstable World*, wrote, "In my later teen years, I had the privilege of being supported by a number of mature Christian men. They spent time praying with me, counseling me, and encouraging me in my Christian walk. I developed a boldness for witnessing by following the example of one man. I established a consistent prayer life by following the example of another. I developed a deep desire for studying the Scriptures by following the example of a third. The more I associated myself with such men, the more I experienced a personal spiritual growth and the sanctifying work of God's Holy Spirit." Christian, you are following somebody's example at this very moment. You spend your minutes, days, weeks, months, and years living out the influence that people have exerted on your life.

Note that you are to give positive and selective attention to those who set the right example for you and others. "Mark them which so walk," Paul says. The Greek word translated "mark" is the word "*skopos*," from which we derive our English word, "scope." Perhaps you have heard someone say, "We scoped it out," referring to a careful and critical examination of a certain object. The word means to "keep an eye on." In Romans 16:17, this word is used for an examination that leads you to *avoid* something, but here, the examination is made in order to *appreciate* and imitate something.

Look also at the word, "*example*" in our text. It is a big, big word. The Greek word is "tupon," from which we get our word "type." The word "type" is a special word, and it has a specialized meaning in the New Testament. It comes from a root that means "to strike," and it describes the creating of an impression by striking the image into a receptive surface. Technically, it was the impress or figure made by a seal or a die, such as the die that is used in minting new coins.

This was the same word Thomas used when he said about Jesus, "Except I shall see in His hands the print (the '*tupon*' — the "impression") of the nails, and put my finger into the print ('impression') of the nails . . . I will not believe" (John 20:25). Thomas was saying that the marks of crucifixion in the body of Jesus were all he had to go by, and all other impressions were not to be trusted. This is the word translated "example" in our text. The example of a Spirit-walking Christian is the only trustworthy impression most people will ever have. However, it is evident that Christians do not automatically set a Christian example for others to follow. Unless we are "imitators" of Christ in the fullest New Testament sense, we will leave false impressions with others as to Who Jesus is and what

Christianity is all about. And note this: *the impressions we make are the result of a die already cast, a Life already lived — and we have been stamped with the Image of it!*

So a Christian must constantly ask himself, "Is my life worth copying?" Would I want to live in heaven among a society of Christians who have lived their lives by the impression I have made on them? The word suggests a "copy-pattern" or a "mold." Close examination of Paul's letters in the New Testament will disclose that this idea is quite common in his writings. In I Thessalonians 1:7, Paul says, "You were examples to all that believed in Macedonia and Achaia." He made the same appeal to the Corinthians that he presents in our text when he said, "I beseech you, be ye followers of me" (I Corinthians 4:16). And again in I Corinthians 11:1, which proves the point we made earlier about Paul's humility: "Be ye followers of me, even as I also am of Christ." There is Paul's guard, there is his proviso, there is his protection, there is his qualification — *follow me, but only as I follow Christ.* In II Thessalonians 3:7-9, Paul put the appeal even more powerfully: "You know how (why) you ought to follow us: for we did not behave ourselves in a disorderly fashion among you: neither did we eat any man's bread without return; but we worked with labor and pain night and day, that we might not be chargeable to any of you: Nor because we have no rights, but to makes ourselves an example unto you to follow us." So the Christian disciple-maker and teacher is warranted in making self-conscious effort to provide the right example, and to appeal to his disciples to follow that example. Like the teacher who writes the "copy-pattern" on the chalkboard and assigns the pupils to copy it, Paul places the pattern of his own life in Christ before the Philippian Christians, and asks them to "copy" it.

Johann Gutenberg is credited with building the first printing press. Living and working in the Rhineland of Germany in the 1440s, he gave to the world one of the most important tools ever invented. Before that time, all copies of information — records, facts, etc. — were made by hand. You see, Mr. Modern, there was a time when Fax machines did not exist! I heard about a man in a Memphis business who was trying to Fax a message to the west coast, but he accidentally got his tie caught in the Fax machine -- and ended up in Los Angeles himself!. Before moveable type, before typewriters, before Xerox, before computers, before Fax, there were people who had to copy documents by hand if the documents were to be preserved. This is the way the earliest transmissions of the Bible were made. The copyist had to be very careful to copy everything correctly. In Jesus' time, the scribes mentioned in the Bible were very important people; they were the copyists who were responsible to preserve and transmit the text of the Bible. The scribe was himself carefully trained for this task. Jesus referred to in Matthew 13:52 to "the scribe who is instructed," and the word He used is the verb form of the word "disciple." "Every scribe who is *discipled*." Intensive training was required for the copyist's technical job to be done well. In his training, the master scribe or teacher would give the disciple, the apprentice, the aspiring young scribe, a piece of paper with the letters of certain words written picturesquely across the top. These letters contained every "stroke" (remember the word, "tupon") that the copyist would be expected to make. The young copyist would practice copying the words again and again, until he had mastered the printing of those letters. *He literally followed the "example" ("tupon") that was set before him.* After he had followed the example enough times, the stroke of the pen came naturally to him.

Dear Christians, all of us are *copies,* and copiests, and then we are responsible to be *copy-patterns* for someone else to copy! We are to follow the examples of worthy Christians until the "tracing of the strokes" of the Christian life become natural and automatic in our own lives. We are responsible to carefully choose the examples we will follow. These examples will play an incredibly large part in making us who we will finally become.

So we see that our text combines the proper model (Paul and others) and the proper mandate (the urgent encouragement to follow their example) for making disciples. Both the model and the mandate are essential. If I only see a model of the Christian life, I will not be able to follow it with full intelligence. If I only hear the mandate, I will think it is too visionary and impossible to receive my serious consideration and commitment. Both are essential.

THE PERSONAL MODEL FOR DISCIPLE-MAKERS

The original model of disciple-making was Jesus Himself. From all eternity, He had been His Father's disciple. When He came to the earth, Jesus taught a small group of men and made them responsible to teach others. He made disciples, each of whom was then responsible to make other disciples. We could say that He not only made disciples, He made disciple-makers, and they then trained other disciples, who in turn would also become disciple-makers. So an ever-enlarging network of trained disciple-makers emerged from the training process which Jesus initiated with His Twelve.

A generation later, a disciple-making leader emerged in the Christian movement who functioned in the Spirit and Vision of his Master. In turn, he said to a young disciple-maker, "The things which you have heard from me, the same things commit to faithful men, who will be able to teach others also." We must see this as simply an extension of Jesus' own life. Jesus said, in effect, "The things I, Jesus, have heard from My Father, I have committed to (invested in) twelve faithful men, who shall be able to teach others also." Our text for this study was written by that second-generation man who was a crucial "link" in the chain of disciple-making. Just what kind of example did he set? What kind of model was he? What copy-pattern can we detect in him? Well, it is very interesting that you asked that question! The third chapter of Philippians gives us a profound portrait of Paul. In order to see the dimensions of his example, let's see what kind of man he was. We will use the verses preceding our text as our foundation.

In verses 12-15, Paul said, "I am not as one who has already 'arrived,' nor am I anywhere near perfection: but I am following hard after God, so that I may fully 'grasp' that for which Christ

Jesus has grasped me. My brothers, I have not fully grasped it yet: but this one thing I do, forgetting the things which are past, and reaching ahead toward those things that are still before me, I strain toward the mark for the prize of the upward calling of God in Christ Jesus. As many as are maturing in Christ, I ask them to join me with the same mentality."

Here is a veritable world in words! Each sentence is an ocean of content, enticing the swimmer-in-training to dive in and exhaust himself. However, because of the nature of our study, we will focus our attention on the kind of man Paul was — in order to see the model he gave, the example he set, before disciples and disciple-makers.

Healthy Dissatisfaction

First, Paul was a man of *healthy dissatisfaction*. Anybody who has studied the life of Paul extensively has become aware that Paul was very dissatisfied before he became a Christian. And his dissatisfaction had been extremely intense! Someone said, "A psychotic is a person who says that two plus two is five;" that is, a psychotic is really out of touch with reality. However, a neurotic is a person who says, "Two plus two may be four, but I don't like it!" In other words, the neurotic is in touch with reality, but it does not suit him. Before he became a Christian, Paul was something of a religious neurotic.

Winston Churchill often told the story of a family who was picnicking by a lake one day when their five-year-old son accidentally fell into the water. A stranger passing by saw the situation and, at great risk to his own safety, dived in, fully clothed, and rescued the child from drowning. The rescuer presented the boy back to his mother, but instead of thanking the stranger for his heroic deed, the mother snapped feverishly, "Where's Johnny's cap?" Out of all the possible facets of this traumatic event, this was the detail the mother emphasized. There are some people, no matter what is done for them, who choose not to be satisfied. They are perennially unhappy with themselves, with others, and with reality itself. I strongly suspect that Saul of Tarsus fell into this group before he was saved. But this is the same man who in Philippians chapter four declared himself to be "content in any circumstance where I find myself."

Any true Christian is a profound mixture of happy satisfaction and healthy dissatisfaction. It is crucial that a Christian keep a wholesome balance of these two things in his life. Someone wisely said, "A Christian cannot recommend the Bread of Life or the Water of Life to others if he himself looks as if those foods disagreed with him!" But we still must recognize that healthy dissatisfaction is a vital part of the Christian life. The Christian has had a deeply satisfying drink of the Water of Life, but he is always thirsty for more! He became an instant winner in Christ, but he then realized that there are a lot of other races to be won and fights to be fought since he got his first gold medal. The Christian life involves a sanctified dissatisfaction as well as a settled contentment. Why? Because, though I am positionally perfect in Christ, I am still very imperfect in my daily practice as a Christian.

Paul expressed this creative tension between positional perfection and practical progress in these words: "I am not as one who has already arrived, nor am I anywhere near perfection . . . but I seek to know the Person of Christ better and better, and to 'grasp' His purpose for me with a more complete grip each day." It is this healthy dissatisfaction that keeps the Christian moving ever deeper into the Treasure and the treasury of the Christian life. Paul modeled this healthy dissatisfaction, and every Christian should reveal it as well. Christian, just remember that wherever you are at present, it's not where you could be. Then let the margin of difference between what you are and what you could be provide the dissatisfaction that moves you toward the desirable goal.

Heart-felt Devotion

Second, Paul was characterized by a *heart-felt devotion*. "This one thing I do," he said. We would call this concentration or focus, and that is what Christian devotion is. Paul was a specialist, and so should every Christian be. His focus was not on a dozen things, or even two, but only on one. His vocation was Christ and His Purpose; his avocation was anything else that called for his attention and effort. Vance Havner once said, "Most Christians could be called 'hypodermic saints,' because they run as if they are energized by 'shots' of the Gospel. They live the Christian life by spurts, spasms, or turns, but not consistently and continually." Then he divided Christians into three categories — workers, shirkers, and jerkers — and he said that most Christians are jerkers whose devotion is unsteady and unreliable.

When a lion-tamer at the circus allows himself to be locked in with all those vicious lions, why does he carry a three- or four-legged stool in his hand? This is not an arbitrary act. The person who holds the chair knows something very important about the constitution of a lion. He knows that when you put several points of focus before him, the constitution of the lion requires him to try to focus on all of them. Thus, his attention and energies become fragmented and divided, and the lion is largely neutralized. In the Bible, Satan is described as "a roaring lion" (I Peter 5:8). Christians could easily neutralize Satan by simply striking on all assigned 'fronts,' on all commanded points of focus. Jesus was a wise strategist when He commanded us to witness "both in Jerusalem, and in Judea, and in Samaria, and unto the uttermost part of the earth" — striking with equal force and efficiency at all times on these assigned fronts. Instead, however, our attention has been introverted into our own lives and our local church situations, and even there, our attention is divided to a thousand petty things — and thus Satan has divided us and neutralized us. Our "one thing" is the pursuit of Jesus Christ and His purpose of total world impact. This goal is worthy of the heart-felt devotion of every Christian.

There is great power in concentration. Let the sun disperse its rays over the earth, and it has a substantial power. But let a few rays of the sun's light be focused through a powerful magnifying lense, thus concentrating it, and that concentrated light and heat can burn its way through a sheet of solid metal! If each Christian would practice heart-felt devotion to Jesus Christ and His purpose to make disciples and impact the whole world, and join with a few others of similar devotion, the impact would be enormous! Paul was the walking model of such whole-hearted (concentrated) devotion.

Heavenly Direction

Third, Paul lived a *life of heavenly direction*. "Brethren, . . . I forget those things which are behind, and reach forth unto those things which are before" (verse 13). Throughout this passage, Paul employs another sports illustration. He sees in his mind's eye a sports stadium, a running track on its playing surface, and a corps of runners sprinting for the finish line. Each runner is exerting maximum effort to reach the finish as the winner of the race and the victor's reward.

Every runner on a track team is mindful of two foundational rules in running a race: (1) Don't look back; and (2) Focus on the finish line. Don't look back! "Forgetting the things which are behind." When hurdlers in a track meet hit a hurdle while running a competitive race, they don't turn around to look at the hurdle, nor do they stop and go back and pick it up. Any sports fan knows how ridiculous it is to suggest such action, but Christians are usually not as wise as hurdlers on a track team. They often stop to look back, and break their momentum toward the finish line. I saw an interesting sign on the outside mirror of a truck. It read: "Warning: this mirror enlarges objects which are behind the vehicle." Apparently that mirror made following vehicles to appear much larger than they really were. Many Christians magnify their past like that!

Paul says that Christians should forget the things that are past. Someone outlined this responsibility toward the past in these points: (1) Past sins must be forgiven; (2) Past sorrows must be forgotten; and (3) Past successes must be forsaken. An 80 year old man facetiously said of his feeble mind, "My memory is what I forget with!" The Christian must deliberately use his memory to forget the past.

Clara Barton, the founder of the American Red Cross, received much criticism, but she bore the burden of it cheerfully. One day a friend reminded her of a particularly mean thing that had been done to her. When Clara's face showed a blank expression, the friend exclaimed, "Surely you remember that, Clara!" "No," Clara Barton replied, "I distinctly remember forgetting it!" Every Christian should be marked by such distinct and discriminating forgetfulness.

> *"We thank Thee, Lord, for memory*
> *To live again the past;*
> *That in remembering bygone days*
> *The fruits of joy shall last.*
> *But for the power to forget*
> *We thank Thee even more:*
> *The stings, the slights, the hurts,*
> *The wounds Can never hurt us more."*

Most of all, the Christian must forget all failures of the past, whether they be sins of omission or commission. David committed several crimson sins as king of Israel, but when he had "come clean" with God and sought His forgiveness, he prayed, "Restore unto me the joy of thy salvation, and uphold me with Thy free Spirit. Then will I teach transgressors thy ways; and sinners shall be converted unto thee" (Psalm 51:12-13). David rested in the mercy and grace of God, and refused to allow a sad history of failure to determine his future life.

In the 1986 major league baseball season, Bob Brenley, catcher for the San Francisco Giants, set a major league record when he made four errors in one game. However, in the same game, in the last of the ninth inning, the same Bob Brenley came to bat with the score tied. Brenley hit a home run for the Giants, and they beat the Atlanta Braves by a score of seven to six! Dear Christian, no matter what errors are behind you in earlier innings of the game, you still may deliver a winning hit for God's side if you will forget the failures of the past and focus on the responsibilities and possibilities of the present and the future. A disciple-maker who stops to pick up the hurdles he has knocked down will never win the race. A batter who is dejectedly focusing on earlier errors will not likely deliver a winning hit. Don't look back!

Then, the disciple-maker must be sure that he keeps his attention on the clearly defined goals of *Total World Impact, the Building of an Army of Disciples, and the Training Process* by which the soldiers in that army train others. Paul followed his athletic metaphor still further when he said, "Strain forward toward those things that are before you." One can see the runner with every muscle straining toward the tape, his total focus on the finish line, and his full effort given to the race. He knows that he cannot allow distractions to divert his attention from the running of the race.

I referred just a few moments ago to a rear-view mirror on a truck. Let me return to that mirror and turn the illustration just a little. A Christian should look at the past in just about the same proportion as a driver glances in the rear view mirror while driving an automobile. The rear view mirror is a handy instrument to have in the car for the sake of safety, but there is no safety in the driver keeping his attention focused through that mirror on objects behind the vehicle! Christian, through which do you look the most — the rear view mirror, or the windshield?

Several years ago, I purchased a book on Greek mythology because of the incredible illustrations it sometimes affords of Christian truth. In that book, I came across the myth of "Atalanta and the Golden Apples," which I have read and studied many times. It is the story of a king's daughter named Atalanta, who was blessed with the gifts of beauty and fleetness of foot. When she had matured into a young woman and her gifts were well known far and wide, her father the king offered her hand in marriage to any Greek man who could beat her in a prescribed race on a racecourse. Many tried and failed, and, as a consequence, forfeited their lives.

At last a young Greek named Hippomenes applied to run the race against her. When he arrived on the day of the race, he was wearing a small sash around his waste, and a small sack hung from the sash. When the race started, she teasingly slowed her pace to let him get ahead. Then suddenly, she put on a burst of speed and started to pass him. However, as she did, he reached into the small bag and pulled out a golden apple. As she went by him, he rolled the apple diagonally across her pathway. The gleam of its beauty attracted her eye. When she saw the flash of gold, she knew it also had a great value. So she stopped and turned aside just long enough to retrieve it, quickly returning to the course to resume the race. She easily caught Hippomenes again and threatened to pass. Again, he rolled an apple across her path, and again she turned and quickly retrieved it. She returned to the race and caught him again. As she began to pass, he threw the final apple across her course. Again, she turned to retrieve the apple, thinking she still had enough time to make up the distance and win the race. But he had calculated correctly, because he breasted the tape at the finish line as she trailed by a step. Hippomenes won the race and the beautiful maiden — and the kingdom — not by his superior speed, but by the cunning of distraction. She lost because of her own folly in leaving the course for a mere trinket. Even so, it has often been the ruin of many a saint in the most glorious race of all that, for the three golden apples of the world, the flesh, and the allurements of Satan, he has failed to "strain toward the prize of the high calling of God in Christ Jesus." The disciple and disciple-maker must maintain his heavenly direction with consistency throughout his Christian life.

Holy Determination

Finally, Paul was a man of *holy determination*. Isolate the words, "I press toward the mark for the prize of the high calling of God in Christ Jesus." Paul is not picturing a quiet stroll in the park, but a vigorous and draining run. Objects held in the hand might not be noticed in a stroll in the park, but such objects became a hindrance when one is running. One of the great tragedies of the Christian life is that many Christians never win any significant victories for the cause of Christ, never capture any enemy territory or troops, never destroy any strongholds of the enemy in their homeland — in short, they never win any real victories in spite of the extreme and aggressive language that is used again and again in the New Testament. The words used in our text and in countless other similar passages in the New Testament are far too vigorous to describe the casual, relaxed, easygoing type of Christian life that is so often exemplified among us. We must not sit back on padded seats in an air conditioned building and listen and look. We must strain every nerve of our moral and spiritual being to run this race and win this prize.

Paul said elsewhere, "The pioneers who have blazed the faith-trail, the veterans that have run the race before us, are like spectators in a heavenly grandstand, loudly and lustily cheering us on as we run the same race today. We must strip down, start running — and never quit! No extra spiritual weight is permissible, and no parasitic sins. We must deliberately take our eyes off of everything else, and keep them fastened on Jesus, Who not only started the race but knows how to triumphantly finish it as well. Study how He did it! He never lost sight of where He was headed. Because of the anticipation of an exhilarating finish, He could put up with anything along the way — the cross, the shame, whatever. And now He's there, in the place of honor, beside the King's throne. When you find yourselves flagging in your faith, go over that story again, item by item. That will shoot adrenalin into your souls! And keep running! It will be worth it all when you, too, are invited up to sit with Jesus beside the King's throne."

In conclusion, pause just a moment and remind yourself of our theme - disciple-modeling, disciple-making, and disciple-multiplying. And remember that God has placed you in Square One to begin the process. Remember, too, that the product of your ministry with your disciples is *to create impact that extends to the ends of the earth until the end of time*. Place yourself in our text — and move out for Jesus.

A middle-aged man and his wife had walked out on a long dock that extended into the Mississippi River at Vicksburg, Mississippi. They had seated themselves at the end of the dock, and were dangling their legs over the end as they held hands and "whispered sweet nothings" in each other's ears. Suddenly, their romantic absorption was broken when they heard running footsteps on the dock behind them. They both looked back and saw a man dressed in a business suit, running as fast as he could toward the end of the dock. They thought he was running to them, but as he reached them, he maintained his fast speed. They parted just in time for him to leap from the end of the dock. With a "wahoo" yell, he sailed through the air and splashed into the water several feet from the end of the dock. Alarmed, the couple raced out to the end and helped him out of the water. The woman asked, "What in the world are you doing?" Panting and spitting water, the man answered, "Do you see that man back up there on the hill? Well, he just bet me a million to one that I couldn't jump across the Mississippi River. Now, I knew within reason that I couldn't do it — but at those odds, I couldn't just stand there and not try it!"

This disciple-making task may seem exceedingly difficult to us, if not altogether impossible. The task of total world impact is indeed a formidable assignment. A world full of lost people is a forbidding concept. But in light of what is at stake, can we simply stand still and do nothing?

Chapter 18

What about Lost Church Members?

> *"For many walk, of whom I have told you often, and now tell you even weeping, that they are the enemies of the cross of Christ: Whose end is destruction, whose god is their belly, and whose glory is in their shame, who mind earthly things" (Philippians 3:18-19).*

In the early verses of Philippians chapter three, Paul has warned his readers against *legalists* who often show up in the Christian fellowship and misrepresent the Gospel of Christ (Phil. 3:1-3). Here at the end of Philippians chapter three, he warns against *libertines* in the fellowship who disgrace the Gospel of Christ (Phil. 3:18-19). A legalist is a person who tries to operate his life (and the lives of others) by law instead of by grace. He operates by rules and regulations instead of by relationship and romance with Christ. A libertine is the opposite of a legalist. He acknowledges no law for his life, living instead by license. The very fact that both warnings are given at the extremes of the same chapter suggests that sinful human nature is very prone to jump back and forth from one of these extremes to the other. Indeed, it is a testimony of the weakness and wilfulness of human flesh that these extremes are found in the fellowship of believers. It is likely that there is no fellowship of believers anywhere that does not have people at both extremes.

Christians are forever expressing wistful desires for a "pure and holy" church. It is ridiculously naive to even dream of such a church. We refer idyllically to "the New Testament Church," but which church do we mean? We must remember that the Corinthian church was a "New Testament church," but it was absolutely loaded with the most lewd and ludicrous carnality. The Ephesian church was a "New Testament church," but it went from a fellowship with a hot heart for Christ to a fellowship which had "left its first love" (Revelation 2:4), and it finally lost its identity and existence (see Revelation 2:5, a threat by Christ which was literally fulfilled). So we must not be unrealistic by becoming more idealistic than Jesus Himself! There was no "pure and perfect church" in the days of Christ or the apostles, and there is certainly no such church today.

After such a caution, we still must give serious attention to such warnings as the one contained in our text. The Apostle Peter also warned against libertine practice when he wrote, "Dearly beloved, I beseech you as strangers and pilgrims, abstain from fleshly lusts, which war against the soul" (I Peter 2:11). But Paul's words in our text are especially tragic and poignant. Notice that he clearly calls libertines "the enemies of the cross." We are reminded again by these words of how very much the cross meant to Paul, and of how much it means to the Gospel and the Christian. According to I Corinthians 1:18 and other related passages of Scripture, the cross of Jesus Christ is the touchstone of human destiny. It is the great divider of human history. It is the great determinant of spiritual life. One's adjustment to the spirit of the cross will reveal his character as a Christian, and will determine his reward (or loss of reward) in eternity.

Our text divides all people into either friends or enemies of the cross of Christ. The friends of the cross are those who have caught the *spirit* of the cross, namely, that of *self-denial*; so the "enemies of the cross" are those who manifest the opposite attitude, namely, that of *self-indulgence* and *self-pleasure*. So the millions of people on earth who are "marooned on an 'I-land' of self-centeredness" are enemies of the central principle of the Christian life. The Cross is the symbol of death to self and sin. By their sin and/or self-indulgence, these people are bringing into disrepute the cross and all the spiritual realities the cross represents.

The text does not allow us to feel that Paul is extremely harsh or hard in his dealings with these people. Quite the opposite. He says, "I have warned you often of them, and now tell you even weeping."

Paul's heart was not only big, it was also tender. In Acts 20:19, Paul reminded the Ephesian elders that he had "served the Lord with all humility of mind, and with many tears, and temptations." In verse 31 of the same chapter, he asked them to "remember, that by the space of three years I ceased not to warn every one night and day with tears." We have often misled ourselves by saying, "Big boys don't cry," but the truth is that the person is too little who can't cry. Tears may be the measure of a man's character.

Luke 19:41 says of our Lord Himself, "When he had come near, he beheld the city (of Jerusalem), and wept over it." The tears of both Paul and Jesus indicate the *tenderness of the mourner* and the *terribleness of the coming judgment and ruin*. When Jesus weeps, crucial matters are on his heart. When Paul testifies of his tears, vital concerns are in his mind as he writes. He echoes the heart and words of the psalmist who said, "Rivers of water run down my eyes because men keep not Thy law" (Psalm 119:136), and of the prophet Jeremiah, who wrote, "My soul shall weep in secret places for your pride." When such a man as Paul weeps, he must have strong reasons for his tears. Here, the reason is overwhelming. He wept because the conduct of these counterfeit Christians was a terrible misrepresentation of Christ and His Cross. You see, every nominal Christian slanders our Redeemer and Lord. Each of us should cultivate a heart that is tender and tearful over our own sins and the sins of others.

The "enemies of the cross" Paul refers to are people who had joined the Christian fellowship, but whose hearts were unchanged and whose theology was liberal enough to accommodate sin. So we will examine in these pages these "enemies of the cross."

THEIR DISGUISE

First, we will consider the *disguise* of these enemies of the cross. These people paraded as Christians. This made them different from the particular kind of legalists we find at the beginning of the chapter. Those legalists were the Judaizers, unsaved Jews who hounded Paul because they believed he was depreciating the law of Moses and the Jewish religion. The libertines of our text were in the fellowship of believers and considered themselves to be Christians. Thus, they represent all of those people throughout Christian history (or in any local fellowship) who pose as Christians, but do not possess Christ. They profess Christianity, but do not practice it. Their lips profess Christ, but their lives deny Him. They pretend to be friends of the cross, but their lives make them in fact its foes.

So these church members are classic hypocrites, wearing an outward mask that pretends something to be true, when in reality the person under the mask is quite different. Jesus spoke of them as "wolves in sheep's clothing." Actually, the presence of hypocrites in the church should not be at all surprising. Hospitals exist for the eradication of disease, yet they are filled with diseased people! Schools exist for the eradication of ignorance, yet they are filled with ignorant people! Churches exist for the eradication of sin and hypocrisy, yet they may be filled with sinners and hypocrites!

Jesus told us at the very beginning that many hypocrites would be found among true believers, and that they would not always be easily detectible. Furthermore, we are to leave their judgment to God (Matthew 13:24-30). Peter was referring to such people when he wrote (II Peter 2:22), "It has happened unto them according to the true proverb, The dog is turned to his own vomit again; and the sow that was washed to her wallowing in the mire." Read and study these words carefully. They have often been used by those who teach "probated salvation" (that you can have salvation at one moment and lose it the next) to "prove" their belief.

However, it must be noted that the person in question was never pictured as anything but a "dog" and a "sow." And that person had always and only been such. Read the verse again to see this. Friends, no Christian is ever picture in the Bible as a dog or a pig! A Christian is pictured as a sheep.

Peter's verse could be called "the proverb of the Prodigal Pig." In Jesus' story of the prodigal son, the boy was in the far country, but he was still his father's son. When he went home, he was only returning to his native environment. However, in Peter's verse, the pig might have been washed, perfumed with "Canal Number Five," dressed up with a ribbon attached — and yet, when given a chance, that pig would still have made a bee-line for the mud hole! Put the pig anywhere but in the mud, and the pig is a prodigal waiting for an opportunity to go "home." The people pictured in Peter's verse are hypocrite church members, professing and pretending to be Christians, but with heart and nature completely unchanged. They may have a "show of godliness," but their lives "deny the power thereof." So they are sinners traveling "incognito" in the Christian community. If they remained in the church, they would likely lead genuine Christians into an abused and degraded practice of Christian liberty. They would lead them to believe that grace covers sin and thus it makes little difference how much a Christian sins! The argument would be, "Since grace abounds where sin is, let sin abound that grace might super-abound!" What a tragic distortion of the Gospel of Christ and of the Christian life! While professing grace, they actually pervert it! This is the disguise of these enemies of the cross.

THEIR DESTINY

Then Paul points out the *destiny* of these enemies of the cross of Christ. He begins his description of them by pointing out their "end." As Judas "went to his own place" (Acts 1:25), so their course leads to a certain "end." How abrupt is the word "end." How final and hopeless! What end can they expect?

Their end is "destruction." Destruction in the Bible is not to be confused with annihilation. The word does not refer to the loss of being, but to the loss of well-being. The word refers to the loss of all that makes for true life, both now and in the world to come. This "end" is the necessary continuation of their chosen lifestyle. I Corinthians 1:18 says, "To those who are perishing, the message of the cross is foolishness." Note that "perishing" is a present and continuing condition in this life, and it merely extends its momentum and direction into the next life. The sin and enmity which caused the destruction continue forever, and the destruction attends them forever. This is the tragic but inevitable destiny of all such unbelievers. Their sin is unceasing, and their destruction lasts as long as the sin. I referred earlier to Acts 1:25, which says that "Judas went to his own place." Does God send anybody to hell? Only in the sense that He enforces the morality and laws of the universe. No, a man goes to the place for which he has prepared himself, and in the unsaved sinner's case, that place is hell. It is amazing that a generation which is producing so much hell says that it doesn't believe in hell. But hell is portable. Millions are carrying it within them, and it is pulling them "home."

C. S. Lewis attended a church service led by a young preacher. In his message, the young man said, "If those living in malpractice do not radically alter their demeanor, they may experience grave eschatological consequences." It sounds to me as if the young preacher knew the brilliant scholar was in his audience! When the service was over, Lewis asked the young man, "Did you mean to say that if a sinner is not saved, he is in danger of going to hell?" "Yes," the young preacher said proudly. "Then why didn't you say so?" roared Lewis.

Clearly, Paul declared that the "end" of these counterfeit Christians will be hell. Tragically, "many" (verse 18) church members will end up in hell.

THEIR DEVOTION

Third, Paul reveals the *devotion* of these enemies of the cross of Christ. They, too, have a god, but what a god! "Their god is their belly," Paul says. The persons described here seem to be of the same group Paul referred to in Romans when he spoke of "those who serve not our Lord Jesus Christ, but their own belly" (Romans 16:18).

Here we address a very delicate matter. Paul said in Romans 14:17 that "the kingdom of God is not eating and drinking." Why was it necessary to say this? Who would have ever thought it was? But these very questions help us to identify the delicate problem among Christians. These "enemies of the cross" were sensual and self-indulgent, disregarding the practical principle that "they who are Christ's have crucified the flesh with its affections and lusts" (Galatians 5:24).

The language Paul uses is startling. They have made a god of their belly. That is, the place which properly belongs to God has been usurped by the very lowest part of their nature. Your "god" is the thing or person that comes first in your thoughts, that you most want to please. To these people, the satisfaction of their physical appetite, and, indeed, their sensual, lustful appetite, is all they care for.

To paraphrase Jesus, their supreme concern is, "What shall we eat, and what shall we drink?" One commentator said, "To them, the table was their altar, and appetite was their god." Another said, "This is the new idolatry: to make the senses and whatever gratifies them our chief delight and our principal reliance." This is the opposite of "keeping the body under" in self-restraint. Yet another commentator said, "What they can eat, what they can put on, what contributes to their comfort and their convenience, means more to them than anything else." Jude described them as "sensual, having not the Spirit" (Jude 19). Like religious devotees, they consecrate their thoughts, their energies, their plans, their drives, to this object.

This phrase draws me up short. This idea gives me great pause. The phrase, "whose god is their belly," presents a great challenge to me. Though I am not one of the "enemies of the cross" Paul describes, could it be true that I have too much of their philosophy and conduct in my life? How do I regard eating and drinking? Do I eat and drink to live (and serve Christ), or do I live to eat and drink? Am I always pampering my appetite(s)? What proof have I that I am truly Christian in these matters? Do I ever take measures (such as fasting) to break the strangle-hold of appetite upon my life? I must give some sober thought to these words.

I found an old English story of a wealthy man who was taking his friend around his magnificent mansion, in which he had dedicated a large chamber as a chapel. The visitor, who thought of little else other than good living, on entering the chapel, exclaimed, "What a great kitchen this would make!" His host replied sharply, "You are mistaken. This is no kitchen. When I have made my belly my God, then I will make my chapel my kitchen, but not before." Some people have no chapel in their life; it is all kitchen. "Their god is their belly." This is their devotion.

THEIR DISGRACE

Fourth, Paul points out the *disgrace* of these enemies of the cross of Christ. He says that their "glory is in their shame." The J. B. Phillips paraphrase says, "Their pride is in what they should be ashamed of." So they not only practice indulgence, they actually glory in it. Remember that these people are unsaved, and they are liberal in theology. They boast of their so-called "liberty," and pervert it into license. Instead of giving close attention to remission of sin, they have assumed that the Gospel gives them permission to sin.

Peter was speaking of such people when he wrote, "While they promise liberty, they themselves are the servants of corruption: for of whom a man is overcome, of the same is he brought in bondage" (II Peter 2:19). Such people think only of their cleverness and enjoyment; they do not see the silent retribution that is always working in their lives. When men glory in things that should inspire feelings of shame, the next move belongs to God. They do not control their own character or destiny when they reach this point. God intervenes and declares of them, "I will turn their glory into shame."

What happens to such people? They throw moral principle and moral pride to the winds and become immoral degenerates. They make a game of shame. They not only sin flagrantly, but they applaud and congratulate themselves and their companions in sin for being free of "archaic and outdated religious regulations which bind other men." Cornelius Plantinga, in his book, *Not the Way It's Supposed To Be,* said, "People who joy in evil show that some wire has gotten crossed in them; their moral polarity has switched. They are in love with death." Tragically, great pockets of American life, especially in large cities, virtually swarm with such "people." Their degradation appears to make them more like animals than men. You see, man must boast of something. Some boasting is perfectly valid and vital for a Christian (see Philippians 3:3). But if man does not know and acknowledge God, he will pride himself in that which one day will prove to be his eternal embarrassment. This is their sad and tragic disgrace.

THEIR DISPOSITION

Finally, Paul points out the *disposition* of these enemies of the cross of Christ. "They mind earthly things," he says. One paraphase of the New Testament says, "This world is the limit of their horizon." One's "horizon" defines how far he can see. Konrad Adenauer said, "We all live under the same sky, but we don't all have the same horizon." This statement of Scripture proves his point. The people described here only have a focus in this world; they have no frame of reference in the next world. They "set their affections on the things of this world"(Colossians 3:2), seek their glory from them, and look for their happiness in them. Samuel Rutherford, the great Scottish Christian, wrote these words to Lady Huntingdon, the British noblewoman: "Madam, don't build your nest in any tree here, because the Lord of the forest has condemned the whole woods to be demolished." But these people are bounded on all sides by this world.

What does Paul mean when he says that such people "mind earthly things"? To "mind" them is to admire them, to desire them, to labor for them, to concentrate thought and effort upon them. Jesus spoke to a man who lived that way and said, "Thou fool!" When God calls a man a "fool," that man is foolish indeed! The word Jesus used is "aphren," which means "no sense." Jesus called this earth-bound man, "Mr. No-Sense"! Think of it — no sense at all! Not merely silly or stupid, but without sense altogether! Why did Jesus use so drastic a description? Simply because the man was totally horizontal in his interests, without any vertical relationship. He was "all soil and no sky." James Hilton wrote a classic book entitled, *Lost Horizon*, and that title would aptly describe these people as well. They have lost the horizon of eternity, and are completely bounded by time. They are like Gulliver among the Lilliputians — totally tied down to the earth by a thousand petty strings.

You may recall John Bunyan's parable, "The Man With the Muck rake." The man in the parable has a garden tool in his hand, his eyes are fastened on the ground, and he is completely occupied with the menial task of sweeping together the refuse that is around him. He is quite unconscious of the angel who is holding a golden crown over his head. He minds earthly things — and misses the heavenly crown! The message is simple — men were made to face God like kings, but instead they are always rooting in the earth like swine.

Note the five descriptive terms again. These people are "enemies of the cross." Their "end is destruction." Their "god is their belly." They "glory in their shame." And the final one: they "mind earthly things." Look at these again, and note their order. The last characteristic — they "mind earthly things" — may seem mild in comparison with the others. But the sentence builds up to stress the greatest danger of all, to "mind merely earthly things." Like carbon monoxide gas, this frame of mind is all the more lethal because it is so often undetected. It settles upon a man before he is aware that his drowsiness to spiritual things precedes the sleep of death.

This phrase, "they mind earthly things," points to the very source of their depravity. Their thoughts, their feelings, their interests, are fixed solely upon the things of time and sense. If they were truly Christians, their minds would have been set on heavenly things. This is one of the by-products of the new birth. "If ye then be risen with Christ, seek those things which are above .... set your affection on things above, not on things on the earth" (Colossians 3:1-2).

We close this study by noting the contrast between "those who mind earthly things" and those whose "citizenship is in heaven" (verse 20). One translation says, "But our commonwealth is in heaven." The word "our" bears major emphasis in that sentence. A "commonwealth" stands against those who do not belong to it, especially against any enemies who try to invade it. This commonwealth stands against "the enemies of the cross" of Christ. The contrast is stark and vivid. They "mind earthly things" and are gravitating downward to destruction; we are "a colony of heaven on earth," waiting for a Visit from our Savior (verse 20). Meantime, we "look upward, because our final redemption draws ever nearer."

Chapter 19

A Colony of Heaven on Earth

"For our conversation is in heaven; from whence we look for the Saviour, the Lord Jesus Christ: Who shall change our vile body, that it may be fashioned like unto his glorious body, according to the working whereby he is able even to subdue all things unto himself" (Philippians 3:20-21).

"We are citizens of the state (commonwealth, homeland) which is in heaven, and from it also we earnestly and patiently await (the coming of) the Lord Jesus Christ, the Messiah, (as) Saviour, Who will transform and fashion anew the body of our humiliation to conform to and be like the body of His glory and majesty, by exerting that power which enables Him even to subject everything to Himself." (Amplified Bible translation)

"We are a colony of heaven on earth." (Verse 20a, Moffatt translation)

The Apostle Paul used a striking figure of speech in writing to the Christians in Philippi. The city had a Greek name in honor of one of the great citizens of the area, Philip of Macedon, the father of Alexander the Great. However, the city had been founded by the Roman government through a special grant of land to military veterans who had served out an honorable period of enlistment in the Roman army. They were settled on land in this locality as a

Roman colony. This served two purposes. It provided a reward for long and faithful service to the Roman Empire. And it established in this barbarian region a community that was thoroughly disciplined and inspired by the ideals of Roman life. It served as a demonstration and a training ground for Roman citizenship.

The word translated "conversation" in the King James Version, and "citizenship," "commonwealth," and "homeland" in other translations, is a word rich in spiritual meaning to a Christian. The Greek word is *politeuma*, from which we derive such words as "politics," "politician," and "policeman." Probably the most basic meaning is in our English word "citizenship." *The Revised Standard Version* translated it "commonwealth." Let me paraphrase the twentieth verse so we can begin to see its full meaning: "We (Christians) have our home in heaven, and here on earth we are a colony of heaven's citizens."

As Americans, we have only to look back to our early colonial history to see the high meaning of a colony. A visit to Pilgrim Hall, Plymouth, Massachusetts, will reveal the English heritage that formed our national background. All the pieces of furniture and household equipment brought by the pilgrims to Plymouth speak of the English homeland. These men and women did not come to the wilderness to live like slum dwellers or savages, to drop their national heritage and "go native." No, they carried England with them. In like manner, our text tells us that we are a colony of heaven while we are living in this earthly wilderness.

A DEFINITION

Let's begin with a *definition*. Just what is a colony? What does it mean to say that a fellowship of Christians is "a colony of heaven on earth?" We can take our frame of reference from the fact that Philippi was a Roman colony. A Roman colony was an outpost, an extension, a small reproduction of the Imperial City of Rome itself. A Roman colony was "a little bit of Rome away from Rome." Philippi was a miniature Rome far out on the barbarian frontier in distant Macedonia.

Every American should have the privilege (and education) of foreign travel. It has been my personal privilege to travel overseas over 180 times. And every American who travels outside the United States should take the opportunity, if possible, to visit the American Embassy in the country he is visiting. There he would see a tiny picture of the life of a colony on foreign soil. In the American Embassy, American furniture fills the place, American foods are usually eaten, American portraits and pictures are on the walls, American customs and culture are depicted, and American law prevails. It is veritably a little bit of America away from America!

Paul was writing to Roman citizens in a Roman colony in a distant place who were, in spite of the distance, directly related to Rome. In fact, there is specific Biblical history that formed part of the background for using this word in this letter. It was at Philippi that Paul first used his right of Roman citizenship (see Acts 16:22-39). Thereafter, he again and again found his Roman citizenship to be a sure protection. After Paul's "Sermon on the Stairs" in Acts 22, he escaped a public scourging by his claim of Roman citizenship. The chief captain of the Roman troops said, "With a great sum I obtained this freedom," but Paul was in a position to say, "But I was freeborn." In Philippi, this right belonged to every born citizen. Throughout the Roman Empire in those days, it was a thing of enormous pride to be a Roman citizen, as well as a thing of great privilege and protection. So these people could quickly begin to accurately interpret Paul's words, "We are a colony of heaven on earth."

Of all people, Christians should know how important their citizenship is. When an American travels to a foreign country, it is essential to keep his "official documents" near at hand at all times. It is essential to have a passport that proves his citizenship. I carry a passport and two copies of the identification pages at different places on my person and in my luggage. Some years ago, I read Edward Everett Hale's poignant story entitled, "The Man Without a Country," the story of poor Philip Nolan, who committed a crime of treason against the United States. When he was tried and condemned, he cried out in frustration before the judge, "I wish I may never hear of the United States again!" He was granted his wish. He was placed on board a ship, and from that time on, "he was almost never permitted to go on shore again, even though the vessel lay in port for months." For more than half a century, he was a "man without a country."

In contrast, the Christian is a freeborn citizen of Heaven, and his name has been written in the census roll of the city, "the book of life" (Philippians 4:3). When the name of Jesus is written by grace on your heart on earth, your name is written down in Heaven (Luke 10:20). The Greek verb translated "written" there is in the perfect tense, which means that it is indelibly inscribed in the book of life and cannot be erased. When you were born again, "your name was once-for-all written in heaven and it stands forever written" there. It is as if God had said, "What I have written, I have written." I am a citizen of heaven, and can never lose my franchise. Do I have a suitable appreciation of what that means?

Let's remind ourselves again of the great contrast between what we were outside of Christ and what we are in Christ. "At that time you were without Christ, being aliens from the commonwealth of Israel, and strangers from the covenants of promise, having no hope, and without God in the world." What an accumulation of horrible descriptive phrases to reveal the non-Christian's experience and expectation! This is Ephesians 2:12; now listen to verses 13 and 19: "But now, in Christ Jesus, you who once were far off are made near by the blood of Christ.... Now therefore you are no more strangers and foreigners, but fellow citizens with the saints, and of the household of God."

The state of Georgia was colonized by a group of English prisoners freed by General James Oglethorp. Most of the men were thieves and debtors who were wasting away in jail. Oglethorp secured their release, transported them to the new world, and when they stepped off the boat, he gave them tools and put them to work building a new colony in America. The experience of these men is not unlike our own. We were all sinners condemned to die, imprisoned by guilt, bad habits and confusion. We lived in darkness. Then came Jesus, our Oglethorp. At great Personal expense on the cross Jesus has led us to a new life in the Spirit. And as we step from our prison cells of sin the Holy Spirit hands us some tools and commissions us to serve Christ's church. We are then transported to that outpost, that colony of Heaven on earth, where we are to happily live and serve the rest of our days. What a destiny! What a challenge!

Rome was known by the Romans as "the eternal city," but she had no right to that title. If you don't believe that, pay a visit to the Roman Forum in the capitol city of the empire and see its broken ruins today! Only one city is "eternal" — the City of God, Heaven itself!

So what does Paul mean when he calls a fellowship of believers "a colony of heaven on earth"? That fellowship is to be an outpost, an extension, a small reproduction of heaven right here in the community where it exists on earth. It is to be a patch of heaven on earth to make earth more like heaven.

The prototype of this "colony concept and colony citizenship" is, of course, Jesus Himself. In John 3:13, He called Himself "He that came down from Heaven, even the Son of Man Who is in Heaven." He testified that His citizenship in His Father's Capitol City remained unimpaired, and that residence for more than thirty years on earth did not naturalize Him as a citizen of earth.

Several years ago, a California pastor named Jack Hayford wrote a book entitled *The Visitor*.

It is a book about the incarnation of God in Christ, and the great "visit" He paid us here on earth. Four times over in the Gospels the Lord's life on earth is described as a visit. All the time He was here on earth, He was still a citizen of Heaven. At birth, He was placed in a borrowed manger. During His life, He borrowed a pillow whereon to rest His head. He died on a borrowed cross, and His body was deposited in a borrowed grave. Whereas John 8:53 tells us that "every man went unto His own house," the next verse tells us, as if in stark contrast, that "Jesus went unto the Mount of Olives." Throughout His life, He was a pilgrim and foreigner on earth — as all of His followers are also to be. Someone saw this truth clearly, and wrote, "The Christian is not a person who stands on earth and looks up to Heaven, but one who lives in Heaven and looks down upon earth." This is taught clearly in the "living in the heavenlies" passages of the Book of Ephesians.

Some years ago, the English-speaking literary world was shocked by the resounding Christian conversion of the renowned British columnist, Malcolm Muggeridge, who was world famous for his caustic wit as editor of Punch. Later, Muggeridge wrote a brilliant spiritual autobiography entitled *Jesus Rediscovered*. In this work, Muggeridge exposed the realization he had come to during the previous ten years of his life that despite all the shortcomings of organized religion, Jesus Christ and the Gospels have incredible meaning for each man's life. Here is some of his testimony: "The sense of being a stranger, which first came to me at the very beginning of my life, I have never quite lost, however engulfed I might be at particular times . . . and circumstances, in earthly pursuits — whether through cupidity, vanity, or sensuality, three iron gates that isolate us in the tiny dark dungeon of our ego. For me there has always been — and I count it the greatest of all blessings — a window never finally blacked out, a light never finally blacked out. The only ultimate disaster that can befall us, I have come to realize, is to feel ourselves to be at home here on earth. As long as we are aliens, we cannot forget our true homeland, which is that other Kingdom Christ proclaimed." What a brilliant explanation of our text! You see, this world has a characteristic spirit and aura of its own. Worldliness is the common bond of citizenship in it. But there is another commonwealth, not of this world (John 18:36), which inspires its members with an entirely different tone of life. Because they have been born into its citizenship, they "seek the things above where Christ sits at the right hand of God" (Colossians 3:1).

In a sermon, the great Scots preacher, John Henry Jowett, used this meaningful illustration. Many English ships once carried a second compass, fixed on a higher part of the ship than the first. For these ships sailed into waters where strange, magnetic currents prevailed, which pervert the accuracy of the compass, and render its guidance perilously delusive. And so the captain directs his course by the compass which is set above the disturbing currents, and he reaches his desired haven. Paul saw his loyalty as belonging to Heaven, and sought his guidance in "the heavenly places," and he refused to conform his conduct to the perverted fashions of the world.

Citizens of Philippi thought of Rome as their native land to which they belonged, in whose census records they were enrolled, whose dress they wore, whose language they spoke, by whose laws there were governed, whose protection they enjoyed, and whose emperor they worshiped as their saviour. In a sense far more sublime and real these Christians dwelling in Philippi must realize that their homeland or commonwealth has its fixed location in Heaven. It was heaven that gave them birth, for they are "born from above" (John 3:3). Their names are inscribed on Heaven's register. Their lives are being governed from Heaven and in accordance with heavenly standards. Their rights are secured in Heaven. Their interests are being promoted there. To Heaven their thoughts and prayers ascend and their hopes aspire. Many of their former earthly fellow-citizens are there even now, and they themselves, the citizens of the heavenly kingdom who are still on earth, will follow shortly. They have received the earnest of their inheritance while on earth, and the full inheritance awaits them in Heaven. Their heavenly residence is being prepared even now. Jerusalem that is above is their mother (Galatians 4:26). They are fellow-citizens with the saints and of the household of God (Ephesians 2:19). While still here on earth, "they desire a better country, that is, a heavenly one; Therefore God is not ashamed to be called their God, for He has prepared for them a city" (Hebrews 11:16). Above all, their Head dwells in Heaven, and they are members of His Body. So they are very close to Heaven while remaining here on earth.

This is what Paul had in mind when he wrote that "we are a colony of Heaven on earth." May God open our minds and hearts and direct our feet as we seek to understand and live by this truth!

DIRECTIONS

If the reader would read the book of Philippians through the lens of this text, he would find some specific practical *directions* for applying this great truth to his life and his world. The Peterson paraphrase says, "There are many out there taking other paths, choosing other goals, and trying to get you to go along with them. . . . But there's far more to life for us. We're citizens of high heaven!"

Question: What does that "far more to life" include? How will this truth influence and change our lives? The better question would be, How can it fail to change us?

When we begin to realize that "we are a colony of heaven on earth," we also realize that we must maintain constant and direct relations with our Capitol City. We must force ourselves to realize that the alternative to "calling home" on a regular basis will be criminal revolt and secession in the colony. In time, the colony will be treated as a colony in revolt, and we will become miserably independent of the Home Office.

What is our responsibility? It is to keep the sense and practice of our citizenship up-to-date. It is to study our "citizenship papers" regularly. It is to read the Constitution of our mother city as often as we can. It is to keep contact with our Emperor's mind through the "hotline" of connection between our hearts and His Office. And it is to discuss together with other fellow-citizens as often as possible the policies of the home city. If I may borrow from *Pilgrim's Progress*, each Christian should daily climb Mount Perspective, fit the Telescope of Faith to the Eye of Vision, and Behold the Gates and Streets of our Homeland. Then, we should use the Spiritual Zoom-in Lens and behold the Person of our Emperor, the Lord

Jesus Christ. If you want to know why, study II Corinthians 3:18 carefully.

Then we will realize that we must defend and advance the interests of our home government on foreign soil. Philippi was a frontier city, surrounded by barbarians, and it maintained constant watch and was ready for anything. The words "represent," "negotiate," "defend," "suffer"and "fight" were well-used words in the Philippian vocabulary, and they should be well-worn words in the Christian vocabulary as well. It is our responsibility as Christians to be "armed" with a tough mind and a tender heart. We must learn how to stand on the authority of our homeland against any enemy who may oppose us. And we must regularly declare the great truths that made us a colony to begin with. What high adventure! We are endangered pioneers in a pagan land. We are frontiersmen in a foreign, faithless land. However, we must never become heartless because of the odds against us. With proper battle strategy and deployment of troops and resources, the battle can be turned in our favor at any time.

So life does indeed hold "far more to us" than mere selfish indulgence or comfortable living. We are charged by our Commander to "live in such a way that we are a credit to the Message of Christ" (Phil. 1:27, *The Message,* Peterson paraphrase). The King James Version reveals the connection between that verse (1:27) and our text: "Only let your conversation (that's our word, politeuma, "citizenship") be as it becometh the Gospel of Christ . . . stand fast in one spirit, with one mind striving together for the faith of the Gospel." The words "stand fast" show the defensive side of our warfare. We are to hold our ground and repel all assaults of the enemy. And the words "striving together" reveal the offensive side of our warfare. In fact, the Greek word is "sunathlountes." This is the word from which we get our word, "athlete," and it is here coupled with the preposition "sun," which means "together with." So it shows Christians as a highly disciplined, competitive team, involved in a heavy struggle "in the faith of the Gospel," always seeking to advance the cause of Christ in enemy territory.

Third, we will realize that every fellowship of Christians is to be a demonstration center for heavenly citizenship, just as a Roman colony was to be a demonstration center for Roman citizenship. A Roman colony was a "Rome in miniature," and a fellowship of Christians should be a "Heaven in miniature." Each Roman citizen in Philippi was to live a "Roman life" — a Rome-centered, Rome-revealing life — out on that distant frontier. And each Christian, a citizen of Heaven, is to live a "Heaven life" — a Heaven-centered, Heaven-revealing life — in this careless and corrupt world. Christians are to live together in an ever-increasing experience of the reality of Heaven. Every fellowship of believers should be a showcase for heavenly citizenship, to cause non-Christians to want to become citizens of Heaven.

The country toward which we travel ought to be recognized by our life. It ought to be evident that we are citizens of the heavenly kingdom by the very gait with which we move about our common affairs. We ought to carry our very climate about with us, as we move in the stifling or chilling atmosphere of the world. We should be like the Dutch lady who came out of a Chicago hotel carrying an umbrella. Somebody taunted her, saying, "Why the umbrella? It isn't raining!" She retorted with a triumphant smile, "It's raining in Amsterdam!" She carried her climate from her homeland; indeed, she viewed herself as creating her own climate in a foreign land! People should breathe differently (more freely) when Christians are near. Hearts and consciences should awake as though they sensed the incoming clear air of another land displacing the polluted atmosphere of this world. And there should be a freshness and bouyancy in our demeanor which proclaims to all men that we are perfectly enjoying the franchise and privileges of the City of God! We should have the air about us that we are heirs of Another World.

If the fellowship of believers (if each believer) could but abide faithfully by these few directions, the fetid atmosphere of the lowlands of earth would begin to be displaced by the rarified purity of the air of Mount Zion, and life for many would become Heaven on earth.

DEDUCTIONS

When Paul introduces the Coming of the Lord into our text, he also draws some conclusions which should reasonably follow that truth. He makes some reasonable *deductions*. Let me mention several of them.

Since Jesus is coming, we may conclude that there will also be a coming reconstruction of our bodies. "Our citizenship is in heaven; from whence also we look for the Saviour, the Lord Jesus Christ: who shall change our vile body (literally, the body of our humiliation), that it may be fashioned like unto his glorious body, according to the working whereby he is able even to subdue all things unto himself." Read these verses again several times before you go further. They carry a great cargo of truths about the transformation that is coming for each believer.

Note the term, "we look for," or "we wait for." This is a compound word, made of the combination of three smaller words. The words are: "receive," "from," and "out of." What a strange combination! We are going to "receive" Jesus "from" and "out of" Heaven. And the One we are anticipating is "the Saviour," One Who is continually doing a work of salvation in us and among us (and He still has a lot of saving to do in each of us!). Here He is given the full title, "the Lord Jesus Christ," to remind us of His full dignity and ability.

What will happen to us when He comes? There are two key words which show what we may expect. One is the word "change," and the other is the word "fashioned." The word "change" is from the root word, "schema," while the word "fashioned" is from the root word, "morphe." These two words were used in Philippians 2:6-8 concerning the Incarnation of Christ. There, they are translated "form" and "fashion." Let me again try to explain the difference between the two words.

Paul says that "He will change the body of our humble state (the body we now live in), and will fashion it into the likeness of Christ's glorious body." The word "change" ("schema" in Greek) means that, in a sense, the change will be somewhat superficial. My identity and essence as the same human being will not change. I will still be I, and you will still be you — and we will be fully recognizable to each other. So the change will be a change of "incidentals," not a change of identity.

So what is the nature of the change that will occur in me when Jesus comes? The word "morphe" (translated "fashioned" here) is the key word. This word refers to a change of constitution, a change of nature. Remember that the model for the change is the body of Jesus. My coming body will be "fashioned like unto His glorious body." This phrase refers to His body as He resumed it in the resurrection, and carried it up to Heaven in the ascension. The body of Jesus was the same body before and after His resurrection — and yet quite different! It was recognizable, but restructured so that He could function differently. My body will be like that when Jesus comes. It will be restructured and redesigned so that it will function like the body of Jesus Christ after His resurrection. Thus, my body will have abilities and capacities then that it does not presently have. Presumably this means that I will not be limited in going through walls as He did or traveling at great speeds and distances. I John 3:2 says, "Beloved, now are we the children of God, and it has not yet appeared as to what we shall be. But we know that, when He shall appear, we shall be like Him, for we shall see Him as He is."

Paul not only answers the question, "What", but also the question, "How." It will take place "by the exertion of the power Jesus has even to subdue all things to Himself." What a statement of Christ's authority and ability! And this is the means whereby He will change us when He comes.

Medical science now tells us that the human body totally replaces and replenishes its physical structure, its molecular and cellular structure, every three years. Every three years! Do you realize what this means? Let me use myself as an example. If I may accept this judgment of medical science, then I have already lived in 25 different bodies, and am presently living in number twenty-six. And all of this without reincarnation! By the way, I heard of a Church of Reincarnation that sings as its invitation every Sunday, "Just As I Was"! And their motto is, "You can't take it with you, so leave it where you can find it when you come back." The belief in human reincarnation is comically tragic!

Let me state Paul's affirmation again. When Jesus comes, there will be a reconstruction of the body of believers to fit that body for eternal residence and relationships in Heaven.

Let me draw a second deduction from the truth of the Second Coming. If we have a proper anticipation of His Coming, their will be changed relationships among believers on earth. Disregard the chapter division in your Bible for a moment and see the connection between Philippians 3:20-21 and Philippians 4:1. Give special attention to the word "therefore" which opens the next verse. "Therefore, my brethren dearly beloved and longed for, my joy and crown, so stand fast in the Lord, my dearly beloved." Note the deep and affectionate relational terms that are used here. I need to stay in verses like this until my relationships with brothers and sisters in Christ are conformed to this shape. What an evaluation of others! What an encouragement of others!

How do I regularly evaluate other people? At the beginning of the twentieth century, the Eickenmeyer and Osterheld Manufacturing Company of New York employed an immigrant electrical engineer from Germany named Charles P. Steinmetz. In the laboratory of this small company, this brilliant, hunchbacked man accomplished some of the greatest of breakthroughs in the electrical field. General Electric Company decided that they desperately needed Steinmetz' genius. They tried to hire him, but he turned down their offer, remaining loyal to the small company that had hired him. The offer was greatly enlarged financially, but he still refused. General Electric then decided that it had but one option. They bought Eickenmeyer and Osterheld — to get one man! Friends,

God paid for a world — to get you! Isaiah 60:22 says, "A little one shall become a thousand, and a small one shall become a strong nation." What evaluation do I give to the one person who shakes hands with me and says, "Hello," today? What encouragement do I offer him "in the Lord"?

If our anticipation of the Coming of the Lord were as intense as that of the early church, the expectation would change our relationships with other people.

A third deduction based on the Coming of the Lord. If we "loved His appearing," there would be continual removal of social and sinful blights in the colony of Heaven on earth. Look at Philippians 4:2. "I beseech Euodias, and beseech Syntyche, that they be of the same mind in the Lord." Apparently, there was a feud brewing in the Woman's Missionary Society in the church of Philippi. Note the tender word, "beseech." And note that Paul repeats it, using it before each sister's name. Paul treated the situation very tenderly and very delicately, with no favoritism or discrimination toward either one. This allows us to see how we should guard all relationships among the colonists and seek to prevent social and sinful rifts in the fellowship.

Let me mention one other deduction that may be drawn from the truth of the Second Coming of Christ. In anticipation of His Coming, there should be constant rejoicing over our blessings in the colony. Philippians 4:4 says, "Rejoice in the Lord always: and again I say, Rejoice." Someone will always reply, "But you don't know my circumstances." Dear friend, look closely at the circumstances of Paul when he wrote these words. No one ever went through such trials as he experienced. He was shipwrecked, beaten several times within an inch of death, stoned and left for dead — and this is only a tiny part of the list (II Corinthians 11:23-29). Paul's letter to the Philippians was written from a Roman prison, where he was chained to a battle-hardened Roman soldier (see Philippians 1:13). However, this letter is perhaps the most joyful document ever written! Some nineteen times he used some form of the word, "joy."

We are not told to rejoice in our temporal prosperity, or in our place in this world, or in anything the world has to give. Somewhere I heard the story of a king who was miserable. A wise man of the realm said to him, "If you want to be happy, find and wear the shirt of the happiest man in your kingdom." So he sent out a large band of searchers to find that man. They were ordered to bring his shirt back to the king. When they returned, one reported, "Sire, we have found the happiest man in the realm. But he does not have a shirt!" Rejoice in the Lord, not in anything else!

If our anticipation of the Lord's Return to the colony were at proper level, we would constantly rejoice over the blessings He gives us. So here is a sampling of the conclusions we should draw in light of the Coming of the Lord.

A DANGER

We cannot leave this great theme without warning of an ever-present *danger*. Though the names of Christians have been finally and forever written in the "book of life," it is possible for a colony of such people to lose its franchise. It is possible for a church to have its "candlestick removed" (see Revelation 1:20, Revelation 2:1, and Revelation 2:5). Read these references carefully and cautiously.

One of the great, dark mysteries of early American history is the puzzle of the "lost colony" of Roanoke Island. In 1587, the controversial Englishman, Sir Walter Raleigh, planted a British colony on Roanoke Island off the North Carolina coast. Because of severe winter and wilderness conditions, a relief expedition went back to England to secure supplies and reinforcements, and did not get back to the colony until 1591. However, when they returned, they could not find even the slightest trace that the colony had ever existed. It had simply disappeared, as if into thin air! To this day, its disappearance remains an unsolved mystery. Even so, a company of Christians may become a lost colony — if they forget their high calling as "a colony of Heaven on earth." Many a church, which could have had the stamp of Heaven's credentials upon it, has instead settled down to lifeless and listless maintenance of the institution and "a form of godliness, but without the power thereof." Remember the seven churches of Asia (Revelation 2 and 3). Founded by the Apostles, and solidly based on the Gospel of Christ and faith in Him, they dissipated into the winds and disappeared in the graveyard of the centuries. Today, the lands where they once existed are largely (some of them, almost totally) unevangelized. It is not a mystery as to why they disappeared; read the accounts in Revelation two and three. But it is a puzzle! With such a Saviour, such a destiny, such a calling, such resources, and such possibilities, what happened? They simply curled their attention back upon themselves, became comfortable, and descended into oblivion. Beware of the colonial danger, Christian!

A DELIGHT

We close our study by observing the great *delight* which was promised the colony. "We are a colony of Heaven on earth — and we look to Heaven for the Return of the Saviour, Who shall change the bodies of our humble state, and transform them into the likeness of His glorified body, according to the power by which He can subdue all things to Himself." Ah, so one day, every colony of Heaven on earth will become a lost colony! Suddenly lost to earth, suddenly gained to Heaven! What does this mean? There are abundant shades of truth and twists of content in these verses which throw great light on the future and final life of the Christian in eternity.

The text contains an explicit reference to the glorious return of Christ. And it forces us to examine it in the same illustrative way we have viewed believers — as "the colony of Heaven on earth." What a thrill it would be if it were announced to the Philippian Roman citizens that the Roman Emperor, the Caesar, was planning to pay them a visit on a certain date. Most of them had never been to Rome, but by all kinds of evidences and connections, they had faithfully aligned themselves with Rome in steadfast loyalty. The Christian has never been to Heaven, and has never seen Christ, but by all kinds of evidences and connections, he has faithfully aligned himself with Jesus in steadfast loyalty. The Manual of Citizenship, the Manual of Colony Operations, contains a promise, a promise which is repeated over three hundred times on its pages. One day, the Colony Of Heaven On Earth is going to receive a Personal Visit from Heaven's Emperor!

Ever since He was here, he has been sending token treasures, Heaven's gifts, to the outposts that represent His Name. The Love-gifts have been indescribably precious, especially since we receive them in an impoverished land, but they are poor when compared with the Lover Himself! The Emperor's treasures are wonderful, but the Emperor Himself will be far more wonderful! The faithful Christian can sing with unfaltering tongue, "Whom have I in heaven but Thee, and there is none on earth that I desire beside Thee" (Psalm 73:25). After all, we are only willing and able to be a colony of Heaven on earth because of Christ. What a day it will be when the Emperor comes to the colony! Have you ever wondered why the early church was such a power for God, and today's church usually limps along at a poor dying rate? What was the secret of their glorious victory? I'm sure than answer cannot be simplified into one statement, but I'm sure that we can give one statement that provides a big part of the answer. It is evident from the New Testament that one of the greatest secrets of their success (and for our failure) is found in their great expectancy. Let a man tell me what he hopes for, what he works for, what he dreams of, what he looks forward to, and he will show me the exact character and nature of his life. Recently, I read Charles Dickens' *Great Expectations*, which is the story of the refinement of false expectations. But the Christian enterprise is entirely based on the domination of Christians by the true expectations. Satan will do anything — anything -- to reduce these expectations. He will dilute the truth of Christ's Return by offering a thousand speculative doctrinal variations of it, he will absorb Christians with a thousand petty earthly interests, he will dull us through temptation and sin, he will divide us through petty arguments, etc., etc. He will say, "Where is the proof of His Coming? Two thousand years have passed, and things continue essentially as they have always been."

Friends, our Lord came the first time after a long, long delay. When Eve's first son, Cain, was born, she apparently thought he was the promised seed, the Deliverer who was to come from God. How disappointed she must have been when Cain turned out to be a murderer! Yet, though Abel fell to the ground dead, the promise lived on. The Promised Seed was delayed a long time, but He finally came. We hold today to a faith that is only partially fulfilled, but when we examine the fulfilments that have already occurred, we have no reason whatsoever to doubt that the unfulfilled promises will be fulfilled. The King is Coming! And He Himself indicated that His Second Coming would be after a long, long delay (see Matthew 25:19). But He is coming! The Emperor Himself will pay a special visit to His faithful colony of Heaven on earth.

Imagine how the streets of Philippi would be cleaned as the day of the Emperor's visit approached. Imagine how the houses would be decorated. Imagine how welcoming preparations would be made. When the Emperor came to visit, new coins were minted, new highways were built, magnificent public buildings were erected, imperial favors were bestowed. A thousand changes were made in preparation for his coming. Then "what manner of persons should we be, in all holy lifestyle and godliness," as we wait for the King's visit?

Notice that Jesus is not merely "a Savior" in our text. He is "the Savior"; not merely one among many, or the best out of several, but the Only One! Can you say, "He is my Savior?" If not, confess your sins directly to Him at this moment. Don't try to minimize anything; confess your deadly sins directly to Jesus. Then repent of them, trusting Him to give you His mind about sin. Then remember that He has loved you personally, in spite of those terrible sins. And He died for you as if you were the only sinner who needed to be died for! And He said that if you would trust Him -- totally trust Him and Him alone to save you — He would come into your life, forgive your sins, and give you the Gift of

Eternal Life. Trust Him today! Receive Him today! Then begin immediately to confess Him as your Savior, Master and Friend to anyone who will listen to your testimony.

"We are a colony of Heaven on earth." He has come into our hearts and made us citizens of Heaven; one day He will come after us and take us to the Homeland. The little outpost of Heaven in this far-off edge of the empire is circled about by threatening hosts of indifferent or hostile barbarians. Far as the eye can see their multitudes cover the land, and the sentinels at the gate might become absolutely discouraged if they only had their own resources to depend on. But the citizens of the colony certainly do not operate by their own resources. They enjoy steady supplies from the Emperor, and they know that he is coming soon to this embattled outpost. Their eyes are fixed on the pass through the hills where they expect to see the waving banners and gleaming spears, and hear the sound of chariot wheels and the blast of a trumpet. When He comes, He will break the siege and scatter all the enemies as straw in the wind, and the colonists who were faithful in their defensive and offensive assignments will go with Him to the land which they have never seen, but which is their home, and will, with the Victorious King, sweep in triumph through the gates into The City.

Until then, Christian, remember your destiny and fulfill your duty!

Chapter 20

A Disciple's Checkpoint

"Therefore, my brethren dearly beloved and longed for, my joy and crown, so stand fast in the Lord, my dearly beloved."

"Those things, which ye have both learned, and received, and heard, and seen in me, do: and the God of peace shall be with you." (Philippians 4:1, 9)

A poor beggar boy had staked himself to a place on a bridge in Rome. He had an old violin, on which he played pitifully every day. He managed to coax a few pennies from pitying passersby, but it was hardly enough to justify the daily effort. However, since his only known skill seemed to be his "skill for begging," he stayed forlornly at the task. One day a stranger happened by the spot, stopping for a few minutes to listen to the boy's hopeless effort on the violin. Finally, the man stepped forward and asked for the boy's violin. The puzzled boy jealously surrendered the instrument. After the stranger had tuned the violin a bit, he began to play a beautiful melody. A man paused to listen, and dropped some money into the hat. The crowd grew, the money increased, and when the man left sometime later, the boy had a sizeable sum. Who was the stranger? It was the great Nicolo Paganini, the renowned Italian violinist! Surely his help was appreciated by the young urchin, but the result was only temporary relief and it was only accomplished through the personal presence of the charitable "minister."

That is one way of addressing the need of the world. This kind of ministry is often done by people who are too ignorant, too indifferent, too mentally vagrant, too selfish, too complacent, too lazy to give real time, thought and effort to human need. Every ministering Christian has probably practiced this kind of ministry. His ministry is often inadvertently a mild effort designed to alleviate his own guilt, salve his own conscience, and satisfy himself that he is engaged in "Christian ministry." This can be tragically true of any of us at any time, and any evaluation of it must not be used as a weapon against any other Christian brother or sister.

During the same decade in which the previous story developed, a little girl came one day to the door of Adelina Patti, the renowned Italian-Spanish soprano opera singer. As the beggar boy was doing on the bridge in Rome, the little girl was also soliciting financial help. The great singer gave her no money but invited her momentarily into her home and asked her to sing. Puzzled, the poor girl fulfilled the peculiar request and sang a familiar song. Patti detected a tiny spark of musical promise (or at least the slightest possibility) in her, and began to give her daily lessons. The great opera diva trained the young girl for seven years! Then she introduced her to the world of performing arts. For the rest of her life, the female urchin-turned-singer, trained intensively by Adelina Patti, earned a large salary and blessed multitudes of people.

The two contrasting accounts reveal the difference between two kinds of "ministry" that prevail in churches and among Christians. One requires momentary personal presence and offers only temporary relief. The other also gives personal presence, but that personal presence becomes an interpersonal relationship by working close-up and hands-on with a trainee over a period of time. The second standard compounds its blessings into an expanding future by teaching and training a disciple for permanent productivity. Thus, the "minister" trains other ministers instead of doing all the work himself. When this ministry plan is followed, the original teacher and trainer works his way out of a job by building others who will do the job in an enlarging way after he is gone. Another benefit of the second standard is that lasting personal relationships result from the long training process.

The pattern of Jesus' ministry, though it began with His personal Presence and often gave only temporary relief, exemplifies the second standard of ministry far more than the first. In fact, the *strategy* of Jesus did not depend at all upon the first standard, but rather on the second. But even the second standard has a shortfall in explaining the total strategy of Jesus Christ. His strategy not only promised large dividends to those who obey at the moment of hearing, but it promised (indeed, *necessitated*) ever-enlarging multiplication through all future generations as long as the process was implemented fully and correctly. The illustration of Adelina Patti, far superior to that of Nicolo Paganini, is still lacking in that it guaranteed no future multiplication. So its outcome finally was also only temporary. Whereas the relief ministry which Paganini rendered to the boy on the bridge lasted only for a day, Patti's ministry to the girl lasted only for a lifetime. Though the second is certainly preferred over the first, *both are inferior* when compared to a ministry of multiplication which may last through indefinite future generations. Herein lies the genius of Jesus' strategy: when it is properly implemented, it guarantees increasing numbers of leaders for all future generations—until the end of time. Not only so, but each follower is to become a leader, and each leader is built to train other leaders. So the test of "followship" and leadership in the "Jesus movement" is not in how many followers a leader has, but rather in how many true leaders he is building with a motivation and strategy to multiply. When properly implemented, this ministry of multiplication will never stop.

The Apostle Paul had somehow learned the strategy of Jesus to perfection. Indeed, he *exemplified* that strategy to perfection. Paul had never seen Jesus in the flesh, but here he was, part of the second generation of disciples after Christ, proclaiming and practicing the strategy of Jesus. Read again the two verses that stand at the beginning of this chapter. Note that in Philippians 4:1, a high level of *relational* skill is indicated, and in Philippians 4:9, a high level of *revelational* skill is exemplified. Here is the perfect balance of a skilled disciple-maker. He practices open, honest, vulnerable, transparent *relational* skills (verse 1); that is, he builds and exemplifies such quality relationships as are remarkably reflected in verse one. Also, his teaching communication reveals great, dynamic, systematic, transferable *revelational* skills (verse 9), such as are remarkably reflected in verse nine. Anyone who can read these verses without pause and without amazement should be questioned as to his sensitivity. I want to ask you to join me in this study in examining the *relational* and *revelational* skills of a visionary, vocational disciple-maker.

THE DISCIPLE-MAKER'S RELATIONAL SKILLS

In verse one, the Apostle Paul reveals *a disciple-maker's relational skills*. Give thoughtful attention and long meditation to this verse. Properly considered and understood, it will arrest and challenge the mind of the typical modern American Christian, and especially the male Christian of today. Strong men are seldom, if ever, heard talking like this today. "My brethren dearly beloved and longed for, my joy and crown, so stand fast in the Lord, my dearly beloved." This is an incredibly rich expression of personal relationship, affection and devotion. Surely the Christians in the Philippian church were favorites of Paul.

The Apostle had written similar words to another of his favorite churches, the church at Thessalonica. In I Thessalonians 2:19-20, Paul wrote, "For what is our hope, or joy, or crown of rejoicing? Are not even ye in the presence of our Lord Jesus Christ at his coming? For ye are our glory and joy." This text proves the point of relational theology by making the two occurrences of the word "ye" emphatic (with *major* emphasis, which means that these words shout from the text). Do yourself a favor by reading these verses aloud, and *shout* the two occurrences of "ye" in the text. Thus, you will see the *other*-centeredness of the true Christian. In fact, in the first

Thessalonian letter, Paul revealed his relational skills when he used the words "you," "your," and "yours" no less that 116 times in five short chapters! Paul lived an "inside-out" life, centered on others, and therein he differed from most Christians today who live "outside-in" lives, suctioning their environment for their own advantage and living for their own survival as believers.

Interpreting the Verse

Let's examine verse one under the microscope of meditation. Paul referred to the Philippian Christians as "my brethren." Go back and read the chapter that contains the account of Paul's own conversion (Acts 9) and you will be reminded of how very much the word "brother" meant to him (see Acts 9:17). When he was in a traumatized condition and uncertain as to his past, present or future, a warm-hearted layman came to him and addressed him as "brother Saul." So he knew the full, warm meaning of this word when he addressed the Christians in Philippi as "my brethren."

Then he called them his "dearly beloved." When we use this term today, it is a completely idle, formal and conventional term (translate, *meaningless*), but not so for Paul. You see, Paul could afford to be extravagant with his love, because he *had an unlimited income. I* John 4:19 gives the Christian's "much-love formula" when it says, "We love, because He first loved us." The source and secret of a Christian's love for others is found in this verse. If anybody has ever known the fathomless depths of Christ's love, it was the Apostle Paul. So he was only personally distributing the richness of the love which he had first received.

"My dearly beloved and longed for." Love never stands alone. It is always attended by desire. That love is far too sentimental that is not coupled with deep desire for the beloved, even the desire to *possess* the beloved. A lover always desires his beloved. He longs for his beloved and seeks the beloved's supreme happiness and blessedness. How much can be done for other people by the ministry of sheer desire! No positive spiritual desire is ever wasted; it always helps to lift the one on whom it is placed. The deep spiritual desire of one committed believer for another person may be like an ocean tide; when it comes in, it lifts everything before it.

Paul called the Philippian believers "my joy and crown." It is likely that the word "joy" refers to his present identification with them, and the word "crown" refers to the future he expects as a result of this present identification. Paul found both his present joy and his future reward in *other people's victories*! This is an incredibly warm relational Christian. No wonder he had such impact on the Roman Empire! Let me ask you a practical question. If your coming crown is comprised of those you have won to Christ and discipled to a ministry of future-generation multiplication, what will your crown be? If your crown is shaped by your ministry for, to, in, and through *others*, what will your crown be? If your crown is determined by your ministry of multiplication through *others*, what will your crown be?

"Stand fast in the Lord, my dearly beloved," is the strong counsel which Paul gave to his brothers and sisters in Christ in Philippi. The opposite of standing fast is giving ground or giving up. Paul says, Don't be enticed or seduced by passing fascinations or by worldly seductions. Don't follow a will-o'-the-wisp. Rivet your hearts to Christ and keep your feet in His pathway. Rest your faith totally on Him, and don't permit any distractions.

Some years ago, I found an apparently "innocent" verse in the obscurity of Genesis 49, and it has challenged me to perseverance over and over again. The verse simply says, "A troop shall overcome Gad, but he shall overcome at the last" (Genesis 49:19). Christian, ponder that verse carefully, and let God build its encouraging truth into your life. Paul later said to the unsteady Corinthians, "Wherefore, my beloved brethren, be steadfast, unmoveable, always abounding in the work of the Lord; for you know that your labor is not in vain in the Lord" (I Corinthians 15:58). This is also the appeal here, to which all of Paul's love and grace and courtesy shown in this passage have been leading.

Implementing the Vocation

Now, having used the microscope on the verse, let's "back away" and take an overview of the basic concept that is revealed here. It is a powerful picture of the relational living that is counseled and commanded throughout the New Testament, but which most Christians today know nothing about.

Jesus established this *basic concept of relational living* as the standard for His followers when He modeled it Himself in His incarnation. Frederick Dale Bruner said, "Jesus' ethic is conspicuously a neighbor-centered ethic, an other-person ethic; it is not merely an ethic of spiritual, physical, or mental self-cultivation. He said, in effect, 'I want neighborliness and not individualism.' " He further established this basic concept *for us* by commanding it in His original call, the call which is clearly stated, for example, in Matthew 4:18-20. Here, He called His first followers, all later followers, and *us*, to a *school* from which there is no earthly graduation. "Follow Me," He said, "and I will make you fishers of men."

It is incumbent upon me to say a very uncomfortable thing at this point. That original school of Jesus was *not a church school* (if you desire to challenge that, just read the Gospel accounts), and for very good reason. If the call into His school is reduced and confined to a church setting, that church setting becomes a convenient place to *hide* from the call, while salving ourselves with a very mild and very tame pursuit. This is clearly evident by moving widely among regular church goers. While a few fishermen emerge out of the masses who attend, most church attendance is for enjoyment, not employment. Entitlement rather than entrustment is the motive of multitudes as they go to church. Personal survival rather than practical service is their goal. Incidentally, this motive is self-defeating, actually militating against its own fulfilment (see Matthew 16:25). How can any Christian leader find great comfort in the minority who are fishing, while the majority are "at ease in Zion?" This standard terribly misleads the majority (it terribly misleads the majority!), and terribly over-burdens the minority. Did Jesus really intend that there be a majority of pew potatoes in church, and a minority of fish-catchers out in the deep?

Furthermore, can this problem be corrected without individual disciple-making? If it could be corrected by pulpiteering, surely the super-churches of the western world should have, by themselves, evangelized the entire world many times over by this late date in history. But clearly, such has not been the case. To see the alternative, let any believer follow a visionary disciple-maker on his world-impacting teaching missions all over the world, carefully examining both the method and the result of the teaching. Today, increasing numbers of motivated teaching laymen are taking up the mantle of such ministries, and the results are already beginning to accrue in fields over the world.

So regular church attendance, while *mandatory and vital*, must be kept in perspective, or it will become the means of evading the vocation. While Adam and Eve hid among the trees of the Garden, many, many Christians hide from the Mandate of the Master in the carved trees of church pews! Nonetheless, when Jesus issued this original call, He clearly and deliberately did not say, "Follow Me, and I will save your souls." He called His followers, not merely to an experience of personal salvation, but to a fisherman's vocation which places clear priority on others. This call does not promise their salvation (that is guaranteed from their first faith-response to Christ), but makes provision for the salvation of others through them. In His original pattern call, Jesus promises help to others through His disciples, not, first of all, bliss, happiness, salvation and gratification for themselves.

I place the question before myself again: Does my Christian practice look like the practice of a vocational fishermen? What is the harbor? What are the boats? What are the nets? Where are the fishing waters? What is done in the harbor before and after the fish are caught? *What did Jesus mean when He said, "Launch out into the deep and let down your nets?"* A church sign wrongly says, "Be a fisher of men. You catch them; God will clean them." God catches and cleans, but He will only do it by using fishermen who are devoted to others. Am I living a life that is "catching"? Before we leave the fishing metaphor, it might also be remarked that fishing is a dirty, smelly, distasteful business, at least in the catching and cleaning. When the consuming begins (note that word; even the fish is caught for someone else's consumption), that's another story! In the Gospel enterprise, the Christian is to be both the consumer and the consumed. Proportionately, he is to consume enough of the Gospel and its benefits that he is able to be consumed without any loss on his part. He is like the burning bush in the Moses story. He is on fire, but not consumed, and the fire is of such a nature that it illumines his entire surrounding and attracts nomadic shepherds to its shining!

The intention of Jesus is inescapable. *His disciples are to be focused outward*—first, on their Master, then on the men upon whom He focuses His attention. As they focus on Him, they will notice that His eyes, in turn, are focused on other people and their needs. So here we can give a loose definition of a relational Christian: *A relational Christian is one who considers the rights of others before his own feelings, and the feelings of others before his own rights.* In short, he consistently puts others before himself. Let me immediately test myself by this definition. Are my plans, performances and prayers focused on others? Read Philippians 4:1 again and see how relational Paul's heart really was.

Some of the greatest of Gospel illustrations, both negatively and positively, are found in classic literature. Recently, I re-read segments of Thornton Wilder's intriguing play entitled *"Our Town."* The young daughter Emily views life from a position of death (she is actually in the cemetery). She asks three pertinent questions, each of which negatively reveals a problem which only relational theology can solve. "Do any human beings ever realize life while they're living it?" "Are we always at the mercy of one self-centered passion after another?" "Don't we ever come close to each other?" Emily's questions are proper, though devastating.

A few years ago, I, along with my son Bryan and my daughter Shari, had the pleasure of traveling in England for three weeks. On the trip, we visited some twelve or more English castles. Those castles seem romantic today, but I continually tried to project myself into the walled lifestyle of those who lived in them. It has come to me again and again that many people today are like medieval castle-dwellers. High walls and deep moats surround them. They are invulnerable and without intimacy with other people. They have become prisoners of their own defenses, and they don't know what blessings they are missing by locking themselves away from others. Someone called them "toxic people," a good title for many. The toxicity of such people sometimes breaks into the daily news headlines like a tongue of flame from hell's furnace. Think of the news that originated at Columbine High or in Jonesboro, Arkansas, for memorable examples. Someone else called these people "basement people" (an echo of Jesus: "He who would exalt himself—even by the reverse exaltation of isolation—shall be abased"). They dwell in low places, and try to drag others down, too. This is *Satan's age-long strategy*, and such people are unwitting volunteers on his work force.

I found another incredible illustration of the same message in an anthology of fairy tales written by the renowned Hans Christian Andersen. It was a short story entitled *"The Bottle."* Briefly, it was the story of a bottle which had once contained a message, but lost it (Christian, beware), turned in upon itself, and became only a bottleneck. The last line of the story summarizes the tragedy: "The bottleneck did not recognize her either, nor did he listen to what she was saying, but that was mostly because the bottleneck never thought about anyone but himself." The illustration is quite self-explanatory!

In contrast to these depressing accounts, break open a New Testament, and see how this ego-centrism is challenged and replaced again and again by the kind of relationships that are modeled and mandated there.

Look back to the beginning of this chapter and read Philippians 4:1 again. These are the words of a man who is consummately skilled in *relational theology*, in other-centered living. And remember that the person who wrote these words is not to be regarded as an abnormal Christian, but as a normal one. The spirit seen in his words is the norm of Jesus and the New Testament. This paraphrase from *The Message* captures the idea: "Live generously and graciously toward others, the way God lives toward you" (Matthew 5). Let the rule ring in your mind: No one can experience true Christianity in isolation or insulation. John Wesley said, "There is no such thing as a solitary saint," and he was right. Paul said that we "comprehend (only) with all saints what is the breadth, and length, and depth and height of the love of Christ, which passes knowledge" (Ephesians 3:18). In the New Testament, true human maturity is a whole-souled commitment to the fullest promotion and fullest protection of every other person. Jesus said, "I am the vine, ye are the branches." *The branch exists for ministry, to pass on the life of the vine in the form of fruit, so that others may be fed.* Theologian Anders Nygren once wrote, "There is no tree that bears fruit for its own use. The sun does not shine for itself. It is only man and the devil who in everything seek their own." Bible teacher David Bosch echoed the same truth when he wrote, "Christianity that does not begin with the individual and his experience with God does not begin, but the Christianity which ends with the individual, ends."

When I begin to explore this dimension in the New Testament, I find that there is no place to stop. The book is scintillatingly full of others, *others*, **others**, and we are privileged to breathe in its rarified air while living in the stifling vacuum of an egocentric society today. Our text remarkably reveals a disciple-maker's relational skills.

THE DISCIPLE-MAKER'S REVELATIONAL SKILLS

In Philippians 4:9, the other verse that begins this chapter, the Apostle Paul reveals a disciple-maker's *revelational* skills. As revealed first in Jesus, and then in all other skilled disciple-makers, the "twin towers" of *revelation* and *relationships* are held in perfect balance. Revelation provides the truth that is to be propagated and perpetuated, and relationships secure the task force of propagators. Without the gigantic truths of Divine revelation, there will be no motive for building disciples and no substance with which to accomplish the task. But without qualitative and multiple relationships in the life of every believer, there will be no network of disciples. There will be few *to be* disciples and fewer still *to build* disciples.

Philippians 4:9 is another one of those breathlessly daring challenges of the Apostle Paul. "Those things, which ye have both learned, and received, and heard, and seen in me, do: and the God of peace shall be with you." Have you ever heard another Christian leader, another disciple-maker, who was as bold as that? Paul sounds like a commanding officer leading his battalion into battle, and crying out, "I'll lead, you follow!" But note that the emphasis is not on his aggressive action at this point, it is on the things he has taught the Philippians, his revelational message. Three of the verbs in this verse ("learn," receive," "hear") have to do with the personal communication and reception of truth. A fourth verb has to do with the vital incarnation of Christ and His truth in the life of the teacher("those things which you have seen in me"). Paul seems to be straining at the leash of language to emphasize the importance of propositional or doctrinal communication, coupled with the incarnational presence of the doctrines in the life of the communicator. Then, he tags on the practical "tail to the kite" —now do what you have heard me teach and seen me exemplify.

Again, let's put this other verse under the microscope of meditation. Let's approach the verse from the standpoint of revelational or doctrinal communication. Here, Paul's revelational skills are *suggested*; in his missionary ministry (primarily the Book of Acts, chapters 13-28) and his epistles, those skills are glaringly seen. Paul walked and talked consistently "the truth as it is in Christ." Here we see the greatest Christian communicator writing of his Christian communication.

The Personal Communicator

First, we can identify the *personal communicator* in this verse. The "me" in the verse is the greatest Christian teacher who has ever lived (discounting Jesus, of course, Who should not properly be called a "Christian"). A master-teacher has a gift from God which enables him to teach, but the gift will never be exploited to its maximum unless the teacher masters the academic discipline which he wants to teach. Paul had spent his entire life in learning, and when he fell by Divine Ambush under the spell of the Carpenter from Nazareth, the disciplines of study and learning took on an entirely new dimension to him. He reacted as if Jesus had spoken the words, "Learn of Me," just to him. He spent the rest of his days exploring and expressing the truths of the Gospel of Christ.

The Propositional Communication

Second, we can identify the *propositional communication* which he refers to in this verse. In a classic case of condensing much into few words, Paul refers to his teachings, the teachings of Christ and the Gospel, as simply "those things." The term, "those things," is a catch-all term which refers to two things: (1) The gigantic *personal incarnation* of Christ and His Gospel in the transparent life of the Apostle Paul; and (2) The gigantic *propositional information* which Paul imparted to explain all the implications of Christ and His Gospel. "Those things" require a lifetime of reflection today. The propositional content of "those things" is recorded systematically in Paul's epistles to the Romans and the Galatians, practically in I and II Corinthians, devotionally in Ephesians and Colossians, relationally in Philippians and Philemon, supportively in Titus, I and II Thessalonians, and I and II Timothy. What an "off-the-map, out-of-this-world," treasure trove is constituted by this body of Paul's teachings! A disciple-maker will never lack curriculum if he spends his life studying and explaining Paul's message. And this is to say nothing of the Gospels, the Book of Acts, and the other documents of the New Testament!

The Prospective Communicants

Third, we can identify in this verse the *prospective communicants* who are to respond to Paul's communication to them. Who are the "ye" in this verse? We glibly say, "Why, the Philippians, of course," but as usual, we presume too much. It is significant to me that when the great devotional writer, Dr. F. B. Meyer, wrote his devotional commentary on the Apostle Paul, he included a chapter in Paul's history entitled, "Ye Philippians." There is little question that the Philippian church was the favorite church of those "born and raised" by Paul on his missionary journeys. The only possible rival to this position was the Thessalonian church. A casual reading of the Philippian letter will reveal that Paul deserved to be heard and followed by these Christian friends.

The Practical Conduct

Fourth, we can identify in this verse the *practical conduct* that both God and Paul expected from these believers in Philippi. "Those things, which ye have both learned, and received, and heard, and seen in me, *do*." All of the disciple-making communication that had passed from Paul to the Philippians, all of the Christian counsel, all of the encouragement, had a totally practical purpose in mind. "Let all of you be *doers* of the word, and not hearers only." "If you know these things, happy are you if you *do* them." In the New Testament, the Christian life is far, far bigger than private belief, official public worship, and institutional support. One cannot say, "My faith is a personal and private matter," and be a follower of Christ. One cannot reduce the Christian life to a one-, two-, or three-times-a-week function in church, and be a follower of Christ. One cannot spend his life merely supporting an institutional expression of the Body of Christ, and be a follower of Christ (again, if you doubt this, read the Gospels, the Book of Acts, and the epistles, where you will look in vain for a merely institutionalized formula for faith). Of course (*of course!*), every believer's life is to be deeply centered in a local New Testament church, but the church is the *base* for his ministry, not the only *place* of it. Every purpose we hold, every plan we make, every possession we own, every thought we think, all are to be surrendered to Christ's totalitarian control ("Lordship" means benevolent dictatorship) and all are to lead to practical expression for Christ's sake. The New Testament word for this practical outcome is "fruit," and the fruit of the New Testament is vast and various.

The Perpetual Consequence

Finally, we can identify in this verse the *perpetual consequence* that attends both the disciple and the disciple-maker when the process of disciple-making is properly engaged. " . . . and the God of peace shall be with you," Paul wrote. In verse seven of Philippians four, Paul had written of the sentinel of God's peace "standing guard over your hearts and minds in Christ Jesus." This is the same idea as Colossians 3:15, which says, "And let the peace of God rule (the Greek word is the word from which we derive our word 'umpire') in your hearts." Compare the phrases, "the peace of God," and "the God of peace." One simply cannot sustain the peace of God in his life without the reign of the God of peace over his heart. And Paul taught us how to gauge our Christian commitment by telling us to use God's peace as the "umpire" or "referee" of our inner lives. If we truly have God's peace, all the "calls" in our lives are going in favor of Jesus. If we are disturbed or distressed in any way, we are in some way saying, "Kill the ump!" and following our own rules. The peace of God is a terribly undervalued commodity in our society because so few have it and thus their only standard of evaluation is the tumultuous life of the "typical" hurried, harassed person. A man who was a proud and pleased owner of a certain well-known automobile said, "Even the worst storm doesn't get in my engine!" And so, when God is with us and administratively in control of us, we can have unbroken peace.

Look at the verse again. "Those things, which ye have both learned, and received, and heard, and seen in me, do." Four of these verbs—"learned, received, heard, and seen"—are *aorist active indicative verbs*. Let me explain that. The indicative mood of these verbs means that they describe action that is to be real. The active voice of these verbs means that the subject is expected to act or has acted. These are not idle words; they are words of full expectation and real action. Then the aorist tense of these verbs indicates point action, or crisis commitment. These verbs do not tolerate delay or postponement. The prescribed action is not casual, but rather critical and decisive.

The verb, "do," on the other hand ("do these things"), is a *present active imperative verb.* The imperative mood means that this word is a command, a command of equal force to any of the Ten Commandments, or any command God has ever given to man. The active voice again means that real action is required in obedience to what has been learned, received, and heard from Paul and seen in his life. And the present tense means that these things are to be true in my life at this very moment and in each continuing moment of my life. What giant words these are! What an incredible chart for Christian living is here! What a picture of a disciple-maker and his disciples is contained in this verse!

Linger a moment longer over the mechanics of the verse. The last two verbs, "heard" and "saw," refer to *Paul's personal contact with the Philippians.* He had been with them, at which time they "heard" him teach and preach the Gospel and all of its related truths, and "saw in him" the true example of his teachings. Here is a vital clue in making disciples. The degree of impact you will have on any individual will usually be in exact ratio to the amount of time you spend in personal contact with him. Furthermore, the integrity of that personal contact with a disciple or disciples will be determined by two things: the character of your life and the quality of your teaching. The two verbs, "learned" and "received," picture the *Philippians' reception of Paul's ongoing teaching* and instruction while he was with them, and perhaps to the continuing instruction they received by means of the letter they are now reading.

Now let me summarize this involved verse in a succession of sentences. (1) Paul says, You saw "these things," the whole Gospel and its teaching, modeled in me. You see, God often transforms me (or you) by the sight of the authentic Christ in someone else. Indeed, this is the way Gospel impact normally begins in human experience. (2) You heard me present (proclaim through preaching and teaching) these things. Successful testimony is given when the life and the lips are united and unanimous in their presentation, and *when they both agree with the Lord!* You see, God often transmits the truth to me (or you) through someone else. (3) You received these things from me, Paul says. The word "received" is the normal word for reception after personal communication, and it implies total involvement of the recipient with the thing received. So an identification and union are established between a believer and the Gospel he has received. God absolutely *transforms* the one who embraces ("hears" and "learns") these things. (4) You truly "learned" them, Paul says, not merely academically, but in character and conduct. A *vital transfer* has occurred, and an even more *vital transformation* has been wrought in your life. (5) Now you must be extremely careful to "do these things." God wants to see these things you have "learned, and received, and heard, and seen in me" translated into productive action. What action is required? *The same action which has been done by a disciple-maker to you, you are now to do to your own disciples.* So here is the fulfilment of Christ's command to "turn people into disciples" capsuled in a single verse; better, captured in the single still frame of a disciple-maker's life. The process has been summarized under five "M's": *Modeling, Mentoring, Monitoring, Mobilizing, and Multiplying.* I heard about a simpleton who worked at an "M and M" factory, but they fired him because he kept throwing the "W's" away! Encyclopedic volumes could be written on the New Testament manifestation of each of these "M" words. Our verse entails at least the first four of these five words, and the process is thus set in motion which will guarantee the "multiplying" phase. Memorize this verse, and let it be the motto of your life. See yourself implementing the receptive parts as your discipler communicates with you, then see yourself implementing the communicative parts as you work with the disciple or disciples God has given you.

Christians are not just patients, or clients, or customers, or solicitors, or patrons, or auditors; they are *disciples*. And their discipleship is standardized by Jesus, not by their dedication, or desires, or limits. The terms of their discipleship are proscribed by Jesus, not prescribed by personal opinion, by any other Christian or by any group of Christians. So Jesus associated His twelve closely with Himself and this association was the heart and soul of their discipleship and learning. By this means, He established the movement that revolutionized the Roman world. The same strategy would create a revolution again if properly implemented by His followers today.

I live in a home which has a six-lane street behind it. Fortunately, we are buffered by a metal and a wooden fence so that we are not buffeted by the sights and sounds of traffic on this wide street. Because of my schedule of east-west travel to distant places of the earth, I have perennial jet-lag. As a result, I am up very early each morning. I drink my cup of coffee while swinging in the patio swing at the rear of the house. During this brief early morning time, I and Jesus casually re-acquaint ourselves and prepare for our "briefing time" together. I was seated on the patio swing early one morning when the traffic on the big street dramatically increased because of an early morning work shift. The street has a corridor of trees on either side in some spots near my home, and I noticed that when a car passed down the traffic lane nearest the trees, they didn't even stir. But when a big truck came by at significant speed, those trees churned as though they had been blown by a strong wind.

Question: How big is your Christian character? Is it big enough to stir those around you? Question: How commanding is your Christian commitment—to you, and to those around you? Is your commitment Christ-customized, or is it determined by tradition? Are you truly His disciple on His terms? If you are, it is inevitable that you will make disciples, and they will be made by specific intent and strategy. Question: Where are you going, and how far? Question: What (whom) are you transporting? Question: Is the vortex of your "run" dislodging others and carrying them with you? If not, be kind enough to yourself to go back to questions one and two, ask God to make them big enough to challenge you, then ask Him to resolve them correctly.

So when the final curtain is drawn over your life, will it have more closely followed the pattern of Paganini or Patti? Tradition or truth? The well-intentioned views of Christians, or the command of Christ?

I pray that the stimulus of this chapter will lead you to linger over Philippians 4:9 for the rest of your life, memorize it, and ask God to incarnate it in you and your disciples.

An Addendum

Relational living requires lingering to discover, to be aware of, other people. At a small gathering, one pupil from a large class said to another guest, "You remind me of our teacher." The other person politely replied, "I am your teacher." Of course, there were moments of embarrassment and apology. The student mumbled weakly, "I sit at the back and can't see you." *There is a difference between faces meeting and persons meeting.* (Source unknown)

All the skills and education in the world will never impress anyone as much as genuine, heartfelt care for them. Plus, few things have a more positive effect on others than finding out and remembering things about them. Knowing a lot about people is a real display of your care for them, and it creates a lasting bond.

People who focus on themselves when interacting with others rarely build positive lasting relationships. All they do is create frustration for themselves and boredom for the other person. Instead, become a good listener. Encourage others to talk about themselves. And be perceptive— when in another's home or office, observe your surroundings. You can discover quite a bit about someone's hobbies and interests by looking at pictures on the walls, trophies, books or mementos. Ask questions about what you see, and pay attention to the answers.

In spite of our human desire for large-scale influence, we really make an impact on *people one at a time.* And we can miss some important opportunities to connect if we dismiss or overlook people we meet every day. Meet others with anticipation, and expect every encounter to yield positive results. It costs little to make another person feel important and respected, but it does wonderful things for him or her. Value everyone, and you will never be guilty of underestimating anyone. (John Maxwell)

Remember, our Best Friend said, "He who would have friends must show himself friendly."

We must learn to look at others ("outsiders") as prospective friends and possible future fellow Christians. (Source unknown)

Chapter 21

The Infallible Sign of the Presence of God

"Rejoice in the Lord alway: and again I say, Rejoice" (Philippians 4:4).

The book of Philippians has been called the "Joy Book" of the New Testament. Eleven times Paul says to the Philippians, "Rejoice!" Five times he flings out his "mirthful monosyllable," "Joy." The joy-note is struck a total of seventy times in the New Testament, and this brief letter is especially full of that note. In fact, this letter could well be summed up in two short sentences: "I rejoice," and "rejoice ye!" The word, "joy," and the disposition of joy burst forth in every chapter, like some underground river which ever and again leaps out into the sunlight from beneath the surface.

Some people conceive of Christianity as the faith of "grinning idiots," fools who practice hilarity in spite of all the doleful facts of life. This, of course, is an extreme caricature, but some seem to insist on discrediting the Gospel by distortion. For example, Mark Twain, who became quite well-known for his skeptical comments about the Gospel and Christians, once wrote of a man whom he described as "an unsmiling religionist who would have made a good candidate for a vacancy in the Trinity!"

A little child was smiling broadly in church. The child's mother noticed, and jerked the child around, whispering loudly, "Stop that silly grinning! You're in church!" He continued smiling, so she slapped him, and he began to cry. "There! That's better!" his mother said.

However, this view is not nearly as harmful as the widespread delusion which pictures the Christian faith as a joy-killing, pleasure-stifling creed built on dark and dismal denials, with no room whatsoever for happiness. Too many young people today regard the church merely as a negative, crepe-hanging institution which continually recites, "Thou shalt not do this, and thou shalt not do that" — a creed which everlastingly opposes every desire and impulse in which the throbbing, surging life of man expresses itself. Sadly, it must be admitted that the action of Christians has often merited such a false view. However, an honest, objective reading of the New Testament will rout such a view in quick fashion, replacing it with the trumpet blast of joy.

One commentator said, "The New Testament is the most joyful book in the world. It opens with joy over the birth of Jesus, and it ends with the superb picture of a great multitude singing Heavenly Hallelujah Choruses. No matter where you open it, amid fortunate or discouraging circumstances, you always hear the note of joy. There is enough tragedy in the New Testament to make it the saddest book in the world, but instead, it is the most joyful." In our text, the innate joy of the book reveals itself again. Let me turn this brief text over like a proud owner might examine a bright diamond in the sunlight, looking for every tiny facet in it.

THE SUMMONS TO REJOICE

This verse contains a resounding *summons* to rejoice. The word "rejoice" is a command. As such, it has equal force to any of the Ten Commandments or to any command of Scripture. In fact, the verb is a present imperative. Thus it is a command to keep on rejoicing as a general habit or lifestyle. So this verse calls for a commitment to a lifetime of rejoicing. This fact alone tells us that we can determine by our choice the presence or absence of joy in our lives. The title of a recent book, *Happiness is a Choice*, is right on the mark. Contrary to what many may think, it is choice rather than circumstance that causes joy to prevail in our lives. The joy of the Lord in the life of a Christian is to be more like a thermostat that controls his life rather than a thermometer that merely registers his circumstances.

The world needs good people today, but along with goodness, it desperately needs genuine gladness. A joyful Christian is a walking advertisement for the validity of his faith, but a gloomy, melancholy Christian is a poor recommendation of Jesus Christ. Sinners are attracted to Jesus by the joy of saints. The quality of joy among Christians is an incredible evangelistic force.

If joy is a command of God, we know that sadness is a sin. Edward Young simply echoed the testimony of Scripture when he said, "It is sinful for a good man to be sad." Pastor R. W. Dale said, "We ask God to forgive us our evil thoughts, evil deeds, evil temper, evil words, but rarely, if ever, do we ask him to forgive us of our sadness." But sadness is a grievous sin! Joy stands like a guard at the door of the Christian's spirit, but when gloominess prevails, the guard is asleep and the spirit is vulnerable to every evil disposition and action. Leslie Weatherhead was right when he wrote, "The opposite of joy is not sorrow or sadness. It is unbelief." The command to "rejoice in the Lord" is a command which we ignore to great peril to our souls.

THE SOURCE OF JOY

Second, the text points out to us the *source* of joy. "Rejoice in the Lord," it admonishes us.

So the source of our joy is not to be in circumstances, feelings, victories, weather, or the attitudes of others toward us. Circumstances may be bright or dark, the stock market may be up or down, health may be good or bad, friends may be many or few, but our joy is to be "in the Lord." Jesus was speaking against the dark foil of the Cross when He said to His disciples, "These things have I spoken unto you, that My joy might be in you, and that your joy might be full" (John 15:11).

This phrase, "in the Lord," must be reexamined with great care. Paul is not simply saying that we are to rejoice in the Lord Jesus as our Savior, Friend, Source of life and strength, Imparter of purity and power. The phrase is used by Paul in a far grander manner than even that! The phrase, "In Christ," or "in Him," or "in Christ Jesus," or "in the Lord" (used here), has a common meaning in Paul's letters, and the meaning is absolutely out of this world. Interrupt this study for a few minutes, turn back one stop in your Bible to the book of Ephesians, and mark all the occurrences of the phrase, "in Christ," in that book. The associations are overwhelming! This is the Apostle's phrase for the believer's full and absolute identification with Christ — and all of the advantages gained by that identification. "In Christ Jesus" is the signature stamped upon all the gifts of God. No human being ever gains any redemptive gift from God except "in Christ Jesus," or "in the Lord." "In Him" we gain the Divine inheritance; in Him we have redemption through His blood; in Him we even have the forgiveness of sins; in Him we are already "blessed with all spiritual blessings in the heavenlies." And the deepest description of the essential characteristic of a Christian life is that it is a life in Christ.

This phrase must be pressed for its full Biblical meaning. It refers to a most real and vital union between Christ and the Christian, between the Savior and the saint, between the Divine Benefactor and the dependent believer. A born-again person is "in the Lord" like a branch is in the vine, and like a member is in the body. So Christ is in the inner life of the Christian as the life sap of the vine is in every twig, and as the mysterious vital power of the body is in every member. To be "in the Lord" means that the Christian's total nature is to be occupied with, and fastened upon, Him. Thus, the phrase entails conscious companionship and continual communion with the Lord Jesus.

With this in mind, we can now begin to see how the source of our joy is Jesus Himself. We can see how we are to "rejoice in the

Lord." In Galatians 5:22, we read that "the fruit of the Spirit (Christ's 'other Self') is joy." Jesus is the Vine, and we believers are the branches (John 15:1), and one of the fruits of this vital relationship is joy. Note the order and succession of this verse carefully: "Believing, we rejoice with joy unspeakable and full of glory" (I Peter 1:8). The word "believing" pictures a continuing activity, and the word "rejoice" pictures the inevitable continuing result of the believing. Thus, if you as a Christian are not in a continuing practice of rejoicing, you have broken the present practice of believing.

This idea is regularly presented in many places and ways in Scripture. Psalm 35:9 says, "My soul shall be joyful in the Lord: it shall rejoice in His salvation." Psalm 35:27 says, "Let all those who put their trust in Thee rejoice; let them ever shout for joy." It is apparent that God expects more than a tame and undemonstrative attitude of rejoicing from His people! Isaiah 61:10 says, "I will greatly rejoice in the Lord; my soul shall be joyful in my God." Note again the terms, "shout for joy" and "greatly rejoice." Look back up the page to the quotation from I Peter 1:8, and note that the Christian's rejoicing is to be "with joy unspeakable and full of glory." Is there anything in our lives which matches the exuberant joy pictured in these words? If not, are we using all of our resources? Are we exercising all of our privileges?

THE SEASON OF REJOICING

Third, the text clearly specifies the *season*, or the time, for rejoicing. "Rejoice in the Lord always," it daringly says. I saw a scintillating paraphrase of this text, which said, "Until further notice, celebrate everything!"

Consider the condition of the Apostle Paul and the circumstance he found himself in when he wrote this letter. First, he was an old man, worn and depleted from many years of toilsome labor and travel. Old age is not frequently associated with an invincibly sunny disposition. Old age has been facetiously defined as the time when "actions creak louder than words" — and the words of the elderly are often not models of radiant joy! The springs of joy are often sapped by reminiscence in the elderly, and they are left full of regrets instead of rejoicing. Others are soured into cynicism by reading the world and their circumstances through pessimistic eyes. But here is Paul, an old man, struck by many a negative blow, nonetheless shouting his affirmations of joy!

But Paul was also in prison when he wrote these words. He testified of "the chain" that bound him to a murderous Roman guard at all times. His life was in danger. He was facing possible death as the result of a judicial process which was bound to paganism and hated Christ and the Gospel. On the one hand, his future seemed to be uncertain. But he knew that his future was actually "as bright as the promises of God." Death seemed to be imminent, and he was dependent upon charity to sustain himself. But Paul knew the actual while others could only see the apparent! In verse five of this chapter, he exclaimed, "The Lord is at hand." This is not a reference to the imminent return of the Lord Jesus Christ, but rather a glad testimony to the nearness of the Lord in Paul's circumstances. One paraphrase says, "Jesus is as close as the fingers of my hand!" Jesus said, "Lo, I am with you alway (literally, all the days)." The day of life, the day of death, the day of judgment! No matter, "I am with you all the days," He said. Sam Shoemaker was right when he said, "The Presence of God enables us to rejoice, and joy is the infallible sign of the Presence of God." It is the awareness of His Presence that allows the Christian to rejoice in all seasons.

Someone said, "If a ship has plenty of good water in its casks or in its hold, it does not matter whether it is sailing through fresh water or salt, because it has its necessary resources within." So Paul often penned words like these. "As sorrowful, yet always rejoicing." "We glory in tribulation." "We take pleasure in infirmities, in reproaches, in necessities, in persecutions, in distresses for Christ's sake." These are obviously the words of a man who models the Christian lifestyle, and is more Christ-centered than circumstance-centered. Paul insists that joy is not to be merely an occasional experience, and that it is not merely for exceptional Christians. It is to be practiced by all Christians, at all times, and in all circumstances. James 1:2 says, "Count it all joy (even) when you fall into various trials." I Thessalonians 5:16 says, "Rejoice evermore." Rejoicing is always in season, never out of season, for a Christian.

THE STRESS ON REJOICING

Fourth, we note that Paul places a *stress*, or an emphasis, on rejoicing. "Rejoice in the Lord always: and again I say, rejoice." This emphasis suggests several vital things about rejoicing: its difficulty, its necessity, and that it can be cultivated. Many factors "gang up" on the Christian to prevent persistent rejoicing. The occurrence and allowance of sin is his life will stifle his joy. After David faced up to his deadly sins of adultery and murder, he earnestly entreated God with these words, "Restore unto me the joy of Thy salvation, and uphold me with Thy free Spirit." This quote is extracted from the fifty-first Psalm, which should be mastered by Christians as a pattern of repentance when they have sinned.

The tendency to doubt God — even about the possibilities of forgiveness and restoration — will kill the joy of a Christian. "He who doubts (doubles his attention between God and anything else) is like a wave of the sea, driven and tossed by cross-currents and conflicting winds." This instability will destroy the Christian's joy.

Lack of gratitude will drain the Christian's joy. Every Christian should be like the little child who "says grace" at the table. The child prays over every item and every person, even to faraway places and people! The Christian should search his life, reciting with praise all of the blessings he can see.

Neglect of daily spiritual disciplines will choke the Christian's joy. Just as a flying airplane needs constant on-course corrections as it moves toward a desirable destination, and just as a television set has "automatic fine-tuning" installed as a feature of its performance, believers must maintain the "diet and direction" of a daily time with the One who is the source of joy.

There may be a Christian reading these words at this moment who needs to heed this point and realize that God has stressed the matter of rejoicing to move him from his pattern of drifting, or excuse-making, or resentment, or cynicism, and set him in a course of celebration, vocal praise, and constant rejoicing. Christians, we will do ourselves an incredible favor if we will simply obey this text — whole-heartedly, continually, and openly.

THE STRENGTH OF REJOICING

Finally, this text (and its context, the book of Philippians) reveals the *strength* that invariably comes to the Christian through the habitual practice of rejoicing. C. S. Lewis called joy "the serious business of heaven." Celebration is a disciplined vocation! Rejoicing may be hard work, but the joy will transform the work. I saw a sign on the wall in the waiters' section of the kitchen at a Shoney's restaurant in Memphis which said, "Pleasure in the job puts perfection in the work." Well, the choice to rejoice puts an incredible number of by-products into life!

Let me mention just one bonus of rejoicing, but it is a big one. Thomas Acquinas said, "No one can live without delight, and that is why a man deprived of spiritual joy goes over to carnal pleasures." Read that great sentence over several times without haste, until you have caught its full meaning. "Carnal pleasures" are a constant threat to the Christian — and especially in this kind of world, and while always carrying the handicap of flesh! To state the principle positively, joy becomes an incredible shield for the Christian against the attack of many a destructive enemy. Nehemiah 8:10 may sound innocent, but it tells us how to fortify ourselves against many deadly enemies: "The joy of the Lord is your strength." Remember Dr. Sangster's description of joy as "the armor of the saint." God's gift of joy is one way in which He secures His people from the sins which deceive and defile others. May God help us to rejoice! It is serious business!

Joy produces personal strength within the joyful Christian. And it produces pervasive strength in the fellowship of believers. Real joy is contagious among believing people.

Two sisters were members of the same church, but they had contrasting dispositions. In fact, their dispositions were so different that the people nicknamed one "Gloomy" and the other "Glory." If people had to call you by one of these nicknames, according to your disposition, which one would they likely use?

"Rejoice in the Lord always, and again I say rejoice."

Chapter 22

Christianity 101

"Be careful for nothing; but in every thing by prayer and supplication with thanksgiving ... let your requests be made known unto God. And the peace of God, which passeth all understanding, shall keep your hearts and minds through Christ Jesus" (Philippians 4:6-7, King James Version).

"Don't fret or worry. Instead of worrying, pray. Let petitions and praises shape your worries into prayers, letting God know your concerns. Before you know it, a sense of God's wholeness, everything coming together for good, will come and settle you down. It's wonderful what happens when Christ displaces worry at the center of your life" (*The Message*, translated by Eugene Peterson) .

If the basic meaning of the word "disciple" is a pupil, or a student, or a learner, then Christian discipleship is a lifetime spent in the school of Christ. And since the key word used for a follower of Christ in the New Testament is the word "disciple," no one can fairly be called a Christian who is not a daily pupil in the school of Christ. Fundamentally, a disciple is a person who binds himself to a master teacher, sits at his feet, learns the lessons of life from him, and pursues in a practical way what he learns. Jesus was referring to this discipline when He said, "Take my yoke upon you, and learn of me." But what is the curriculum in Christ's classroom?

There are a lot of lifetime lessons to be learned in the school of Christ, but there are some that seem to be much more important than others. One of these major lessons is in our text for this study. If a disciple of Christ would live, moment by moment, on the basis of this foundational text, many of his problems would be resolved and many of the seemingly elusive Christian benefits would automatically become his. Remember, the school is the entire discipline of Christian discipleship. The student is the individual Christian. Christ's school is like any other school in that there is a difference in the appreciation, apprehension and appropriation among the students, but the ideal is the same in all cases — the full education, full enjoyment and full employment of each student in the school. The scholar who often teaches the "classes" and the "lessons" is the person who has excelled in the particular discipline in question. And the standard is the revealed truth of the New Testament. Our text gives us one of the most important standard lessons in the entire school. This is "Christianity 101." Here we will learn the first fundamentals of faith. Here we will see an ideal portrait of a disciple of Christ. We may have to take the course again and again before we get a passing grade, but this is basic.

It is instructive to note as we approach this text that it occurs in Paul's letter to the Philippians. The city of Philippi was a Roman colony, and since it was a frontier colony, there was a garrison of Roman soldiers kept in occupation there. Undoubtedly, Paul's readers had seen many a time the troop movements of this garrison of soldiers in and around the city. Using this background for his illustration and idea, Paul presented one of the greatest lessons of faith that can be learned. We will seek to understand it as the Philippian readers themselves might have heard it.

There are *three primary symbols* underlying the truths of this passage. First is the symbol of a *citadel*, or a fortress. In Paul's statement, the citadel is a symbol of "your hearts and minds." Your heart and mind make up a vast sprawling complex within you, like a vast fortress. Have you ever thought of your heart and mind as a vast military establishment? Well, they are! Your inner life is the battleground between good and evil. The old Puritans spoke of your inner life as "the Empire of the Soul." This means that, however obscure you may seem to yourself and to others, you are really a vast inner empire, whose frontiers range further than you have ever explored and whose affairs of state are far more complex than you have ever imagined.

The second military symbol used in these verses is that of a *siege*. The fact that a guard is needed (which we will see in just a moment) means that the enemy is near, and either may make a real attack, or has already done so. The idea of this text is that an entire enemy army surrounds the fortress and is seeking to infiltrate and destroy it. Your heart and your mind are surrounded by an army of subtle enemies, always seeking to gain an entrance and assume control within you. Anxiety, fear, doubt, temptation, sin, sorrow — these and many more are at the gate, cunningly watching, waiting and working for admission. The siege is made by all the factors of life that oppose Christian experience.

The final military symbol of the text is that of a *sentry* who patrols the gates. A sentinel is patrolling the life of a committed Christian, guarding the entrances. And this sentry, properly stationed, will hold the fort against every threatening intruder. In the illustration, the sentry is the peace of God. The peace of God, like some mighty sentinel angel, goes to and fro before the gate of our inner life, keeping back all intruders who would break in upon the affections and thoughts and capture them. Do you see how vast and important this text is? Now we will examine this lesson from the "Christian's First Reader" in the "Christianity 101" curriculum more closely.

A PROHIBITION

The lesson begins with a *prohibition*. It does not open negatively because God delights in imposing restrictions on our lives, but because the thing cautioned against is one of the most serious and widespread dangers in the Christian life. "Be anxious for nothing," it says. The words "anxious" and "anxiety" come from the same root as the word "anger," and this root word refers to the physical act of choking. So Paul is writing here about something that chokes the life of faith. Most modern translations of the Bible translate the statement, "Don't worry about anything," and this translation places us on far more understandable ground. This command is an echo of one of the crucial sections of Jesus' Sermon on the Mount (Matthew 6:25-34), a passage which requires a lifetime of study and review. Both passages deal with a common and deadly sin among Christians. In fact, this sin is so common that Alexander Maclaren, the great Scottish pastor, called this command "the impossible injunction."

A recent "Luann" cartoon in the Sunday newspaper recorded a conversation between Luann and her older brother. With a downcast look and head cupped in her hands, Luann says, "I'm worried about this math test I have tomorrow, Brad." Brad responds, "Hey, welcome to 'Worry School,' Luann." Then he adds, "But you're just at the start of your worries. You're only in 'Beginning Worry.' Next, you'll move up to 'Intermediate Worry' — dating, puberty, greasy hair. Then comes 'Advanced Worry' — money, car, career. That's where I am. After that, you pick a couple of worries to major in. Dad's are the arms race and hair loss. Mom's are wrinkles and the ozone layer. But you know what's the biggest worry in 'Worry School,' Luann?" Luann asks, "What?" Brad leans over her threateningly and replies, "You never graduate!" Maclaren's title for this command, "the impossible injunction," seems to be accurate, doesn't it?

The Desperate Waste

The Bible points out the *desperate waste of worry*. Psychologist Wayne Dyer describes worry and guilt as "the two great wastes" of life. He is very likely correct, but for our purposes in this study, guilt will have to stand in line and wait its turn to be the subject of another study. Worry is the subject of this one. Worry is such a waste! It irritates the spirit, ruffles the temper, upsets the balance of life, sponsors moodiness, sharpness and anger, sets a man at war with himself, his neighbor, God's providence and God's appointments — and what good has it ever done? What good could it possibly do? None whatever. It is a desperate waste of time, energy, health, creative possibilities, even of life itself.

Robert Burns, the quaint Scottish poet, put the dilemma in these vivid words:

> "*Human beings are such fools,*
> "*For all their colleges and schools,*
> *That when no real ills perplex them,*
> *They manufacture enough themselves to vex them."*

The Deadly Wickedness

Furthermore, the Bible points out the *deadly wickedness of worry*. It clearly declares that worry is atheistic in nature and turns a Christian into a practical heathen (Matthew 6:31-32). John Henry Jowett, another great Scottish preacher, said, "Worry is an alloy which always debases the fine metal of Christian character." If these things are true, then our lives are characterized by desperate waste and deadly wickedness far more often than we think.

Several years ago, the Hayden Planetarium decided to have some fun and to educate the public at the same time, so it offered to take reservations for imaginary space trips. The sponsors were shocked when applications rolled in by the thousands. Finally, someone concluded that so many people applied for the trips because they wanted a chance, even though it was only an imaginary one, to escape from all their troubles and worries. In fact, one applicant wrote, "It would be heaven to get away from this troubled earth and to go some place where I wouldn't have to worry." Let me say quickly, before there is a fresh run on Hayden Planetarium and everyone tries to get a ticket to Mars, that you cannot run away from your worries. One woman spoke for many of us when she exclaimed, "Don't tell me it doesn't do any good to worry. Most of the things I worry about never happen!" Dear friend, the worry is within you, and if you are to get rid of it, you must attack it at its source. And that is precisely what Paul's statement is all about.

Among other things, it offers a battle-tested formula for overcoming worry.

Note that the brief prohibition that opens this passage, "Don't worry about anything," is followed abruptly by the word "but." Paul is turning a corner through that contradictory conjunction "but." He is moving from the negative prohibition to the positive counsel of the passage. The word "but" implies that what follows is the sure preventive, the sure preservative, against the "worrywart" disposition that tempts all of us. On the two sides of the word "but" in this paragraph of Scripture, Paul constructs the two alternatives of life. And it must be clearly understood that these are the only two alternatives of life. This means that if you do not take the one course, you are sure to take the other. If a man does not pray about everything, he will be worried about most things.

Like Martha of old, the man who does not pray about everything will be "worried and troubled about many, many things," when he might be like Mary, about whom Jesus said, "One thing is needful, and Mary has chosen the better course, which shall not be taken from her" (Luke 10:38-42). Martha was dominated by the formula, "Hurry, scurry, worry — and bury!" while "Mary sat at Jesus' feet, and heard His Word" (verse 39). That story provides a dramatic illustration of the two alternatives presented in our text.

Martin Luther, with his usual clear perception and rough speech, said that each man's heart contains two millstones. If the man doesn't put something between them to grind, they will grind each other. God is the buffer, and the peace of God is the benefit! It is because God is not in his proper place in a practical way in our hearts that the two stones rub the surface off of each other and release incredible friction into our total beings. The only opponent which will win over worry is trust, and the only way to turn wicked and wasteful worry out of my heart is to usher God into it, and keep him resolutely in it — on His terms and according to the formula of our text. So now we will explore that formula.

THE PRESCRIPTION

Having "cleared the heart" through the negative prohibition, Paul now offers the *positive prescription* which will fill it with the serenity of heaven. "In everything by prayer and supplication with thanksgiving, let your requests be made known unto God." The total prescription could be summarized in three sentences: Be careful for nothing. Be prayerful about everything. Be thankful for anything.

Picture three circles on a page. Place the word WORRY under one of the circles, the word PRAYER under the second circle, and the word THANKSGIVING under the third circle. Inside the "Worry" circle, put the word, Nothing. Inside the "Prayer" circle, put the word, Everything. Inside the "Thanksgiving" circle, put the word, Anything. It would probably make this text more vivid in your mind if you actually drew these circles on a page and put the appropriate words beneath and within each circle.

Be Careful For Nothing

"Be careful for nothing." "Don't worry about anything." Since the entire first point of this study was devoted to this prohibition, I will only mention here a few additional ideas. This negative precept is not an encouragement to be light-hearted and indifferent. This is not an encouragement to be "careless" in the bad sense of that word. Nor is it an encouragement to omit forethought from your life. It was said of Jesus Himself that "for the joy that was set before Him, He endured the cross, despising the shame, and is set down on the right hand of God."

No, this is merely very timely counsel for dealing with a real enemy of the Christian life. Jesus recognized the importance of this by devoting a substantial part of the Sermon on the Mount to the subject — one-seventh of it, to be exact. This is a worry-weary world, and Christians are laden with the burden of worry, as well as lost people.

A Sunday School teacher was teaching the story of Elijah being caught up into heaven in a chariot of fire. She was doing everything she knew to capture the attention, the minds and the hearts of the young boys in her class. She asked, "Jimmy, would you like to ride to heaven in a chariot of fire?" The boy blurted out his response: "Yes, if God was driving." This text tells us how to get God in the driver's seat of our lives. But first, it is necessary to be sure that wicked worry is not in a position to wreck the vehicle. "Be careful for nothing."

Be Prayerful About Everything

"In everything by prayer and supplication . . ., let your requests be made known unto God." There are three specialized words used in this statement for various aspects of prayer. The word *"prayer"* refers to prayer in general. The word *"supplication"* refers to prayer in particular. And the word *"request"* refers to prayer in detail. These three words go from general prayer, to more specific prayer, to very specific prayer. The first word points out the indispensable nature of prayer as an activity of the Godly life. The second and third words encourage us to keep every detail of our lives before God for His attention and blessing, and for our growth and gratification. "Prayer instead of care" would be a worthy motto to inscribe over every Christian life. It is a rule of life that the careful person is not a prayerful person, and the prayerful person is not a careful person. It can easily be practically proven in any man's life that as prayer advances, care retreats.

Note that significant prepositional phrase, "in everything." Has it ever come home to you as a personal discovery that you can talk to God about absolutely anything — anything whatever that is burdening your secret soul? Indeed, that is what God desires, not stereotyped prayers daily following a beaten track (and with the same vocabulary), nor vague generalities which only skim the surface of the real difficulty or problem, but your most intimate confidence about everything. Remember that, though you are coming to God's throne, it is a "throne of grace." It is identified as a "mercy seat" (and the blood of God's dear Son has opened the way to it!), and you cannot bring anything to God that His mercy (and the blood of Christ) cannot cover.

The other words for prayer in this statement, "supplication" and "requests" move us from the general exercise of prayer to the most minute particulars in prayer. Two things are included in the word "supplication": human need, and the desire to have the need met. The word itself means "an appeal for supply," hence "supply-cation." Then follows the word "requests," and this word is coupled with a possessive pronoun, "your requests." So your prayer is not to be a mere repetition of a prayer-lesson you have learned in what Andrew Murray called "the school of prayer." True prayer is not a rote repetition, but a romance relationship. What tricks the enemy plays on us at this point! Just listen to God's people pray. The prayers are so formal, so predictable, so prosaic! If a man were to talk to his wife with the vocabulary and poor creativity he uses in prayer, she would likely tell him to take a walk! I cannot imagine the conversational exchange of lovers sounding like the usual prayers of Christians. Also, this statement lays to rest our fears that our prayers may be too selfish. Jesus set a child before the people and said, "Let my disciples develop the simplicity of this child." A child's requests are for its own needs. Obviously, this course in "Christianity 101" must be accompanied by other courses, such as "Basic Intercession" and "Inside-Out Living" and "Foundational Self-Denial." Meanwhile, let's learn this first lesson well. "Tell God every detail of your needs in earnest prayer," the Phillips paraphrase says.

Be Thankful For Anything

"In everything by prayer and supplication with thanksgiving, let your requests be made known unto God." Here is another powerful prepositional phrase that conditions the exercise of prayer. *"With thanksgiving."* The addition of this clause seems to suggest that we are very prone to omit this ingredient, and that the omission will drain the vitality out of our prayers. Thanksgiving should be regarded as the Siamese twin of prayer.

> *"Prayers and praises should always go in pairs,*
> *They should always bring praises who offer prayers."*

One of the things I often heard my mother say was, "What do you say?" "What do you say to the nice man?" "What do you say to the lady?" Every time someone gave me a gift, a favor, a compliment or a kindness, I would hear it again: "What do you say?" I discovered that this was not really a question; it was a strong suggestion — even a command! Being translated, it meant, "Be sure to say 'Thank you'." The problem usually was that, though I answered properly, the answer was mechanical. It did not represent real thanksgiving; it was merely the paying of an acknowledged debt.

I fear that we often learn this lesson in our Christian curriculum studies in the same manner. We learn about prayer, and that compliments are a good part of any growing relationship. Then we thank God — because we have learned that we are supposed to. It would be far wiser to examine the goodness of God and rehearse the blessings of God until thanksgiving becomes a spontaneous act in our prayers. I like the cartoon in which a parent explains to a neighbor, "I never saw a kid with so many blessings. He was counting them on his hand-calculator and the batteries went dead!" We are the recipients of so many blessings that to think of them should lead to thanksgiving for them.

How much poorer prayer is when not attended by thanksgiving, and how much richer it is when thanksgiving is included! The old adage, "To think is to thank," is surely true. Think of the positive blessings we have received throughout our lives. God has "daily loaded us with benefits" (Psalm 68:19). Then, think of the negative blessings we have received, without which we could not have survived. Every misery you haven't got is a mercy you have got! We can count our positive blessings, but we can only count our negative blessings by examining all the misery in the world and realizing that those things do not describe us! Should thanksgiving not spring from our lives like a fountain?

Many years ago, when Rudyard Kipling was one of the more popular writers of his time, it was reported that he received ten shillings for every word he wrote. Some students at Oxford University, less impressed with his success than they should have been, sent Kipling ten shillings with the request that he send them "one of your very best words." He cabled back: "Thanks." That is one of the very best words in any language, and it is worth so much both to the man who speaks it and to the man who hears it. When thanksgiving attends prayer, it is worth so much both to the man who prays and to the God Who hears prayer.

This part of the formula ("with thanksgiving") would be especially meaningful to the member of the Philippian church. When Paul first went to Philippi and began to minister there, he and his missionary partner Silas were arrested and put in a Roman jail there. They were beaten and their feet were fastened in stocks, but "at midnight Paul and Silas prayed and sang praises unto God" (Acts 16:15). The jailer who was converted at midnight in that Roman prison that night was probably still a member of the Philippian church when Paul wrote this letter to them, and he would be able to say an "amen" to the "thanksgiving" clause in Paul's statement because he had seen Paul practice then what he was preaching now.

On one occasion ten lepers came to Christ with a supplication for healing. He granted their request. But only one of the ten returned to express thanksgiving. Only one completed the cycle and answered the getting of mercy by the giving of praise. The weight of God's mercies pressing down on the healed Samaritan, finding him spiritually alive, pressed his thanksgiving up to the throne. But the same weight pressing upon the other nine, finding them spiritually dull and dead, did not move them upwards at all. Christian, just because you are alive in Christ, have been delivered from the deadly leprosy of sin, and have been unspeakably blessed, "in everything give thanks, for this is the will of God in Christ Jesus concerning you" (I Thess 5:18). Be thankful for anything.

Here, then, is a trinity of trust that will transform a believer's life: Be careful for nothing; be prayerful about everything; be thankful for anything. This prescription will invariably deliver the practitioner from worry and into victory.

THE PRODUCT

When a Christian obeys the prohibition and follows the prescription, he may look for the *product*. A certain outcome has been promised. "And the peace of God, which passeth all understanding, shall keep your hearts and minds through Christ Jesus."

The Sequence

Note the *sequence* pictured in the word "and." As the day follows the night, as your body always casts a shadow when you stand in the sunshine, this product will follow the fulfillment of the prescription. If you are careful for nothing, prayerful about everything, and thankful for anything, this result will follow. It seems that the promise of peace is invariably conditional in Scripture. "Being justified by faith we have peace with God" (Romans 5:1). "To be spiritually minded is life and peace" (Romans 8:6). "Great peace have they who love Thy law" (Psalm 119:165). "Thou wilt keep him in perfect peace whose mind is stayed on Thee" (Isaiah 26:3). So this peace is conditional; it is present when the conditions are met.

The Security

Note also the *security* of this peace. "The peace of God . . . will keep your hearts and minds in Christ Jesus." The peace of God will keep us from sinning under our temptations, and will keep us from sinking under our troubles. As wonderful as that is, we will miss an incredible blessing if we miss the meaning of the terms that are used here. The key word is the word "keep." It is a military word, and majors on the military status of the city of Philippi as a Roman colony. The word means to "guard as with a garrison" of soldiers.

The word "keep" is used in only four places in the New Testament. It is used in II Corinthians 11:32 in a setting where the officials of the city of Damascus were trying to capture the Apostle Paul. Paul later wrote, "In Damascus the governor under Aretas the king kept the city of the Damascenes with a garrison, desirous to arrest me." The word translated "kept with a garrison" is the same as the word used in our text.

Then the word is used in Galatians 3:23, where Paul said, "Before faith came, we (Christians) were kept under the law (as if the law were our jailer), shut up ('imprisoned") unto the faith which should afterward be revealed." The word translated "we were kept" is the same root word as the word "keep" in our text. We were "guarded as with a garrison" under the law before we came to Christ. Then the word is used in I Peter 1:5, which says that saved people "are kept ('guarded as with a garrison') by the power of God through faith unto salvation." So our salvation is eternally secure because it is guarded by the omnipotence of God.

Now we can clearly see the product of learning the lesson and pursuing the prescription of our text. The inner peace that is promised here is quite different from what many people imagine. Many believers expect deliverance *from* conflict, persecution, hostility, danger and misunderstanding, but instead, we are promised deliverance *in* these things. "In all these things we are more than conquerors through Him who loves us" (Romans 8:37). "When thou passest through the waters, I will be with thee; and through the rivers, they shall not overflow thee: when thou walkest through the fire, thou shalt not be burned; neither shall the flame kindle upon thee" (Isaiah 43:2). Note that we are delivered *in* the difficulty and through it, but we may not be delivered *from* it. The peace of God guards us in the midst of battle. No wonder he says that this peace of God "passes all understanding" (and misunderstanding, also, we might add)!

Two artists sought to see which could paint the picture that best revealed the idea of peace. One of them painted a picture of a beautiful lake high in the mountains. It was a beautiful and peaceful sight. Not a ripple stirred the water. There was not a bird in the sky. Not a leaf drifted down in the breeze. There was no indication of movement in the picture at all. If you have ever been out on a lake early in the morning "before Mother Nature begins to awaken her household," you know what a peaceful sight it is.

But the other artist had painted a picture of a roaring waterfall; reaching far out over the waterfall was the limb of a mighty oak. Cradled on this limb was a little sparrow, sitting on her nest. There, surrounded by what seemed to be terrible danger, in the midst of the roar of the waterfall and almost in the spray from the fall, the little sparrow sat upon her nest as though she had not a care in the world. Her nest was cradled on the limb of a mighty oak. Even so, the peace which the Christian has found is not for some idyllic time in some perfect place; it is for here and now in the midst of all the trials and troubles and tribulations of this life. One person said humorously, "When God gives you tribulations, it would appear that He expects you to tribulate." But amid the tribulations, you will be fortified by the tranquility of God — if you learn the lesson of Christianity 101 and follow its prescription.

I read somewhere that no matter how violently the winds may blow nor how high the waves may roll on the surface of the sea, down in the depths of the sea it is always calm and quiet and still. Surface boats will have to weather the storm, but the passengers in a submarine simply abide as the vessel sits in the calm on the bottom of the sea until the storm is past. Will we be surface saints who are rocked and blown about and torn apart by the high winds of life, or will we be submarine saints who maintain calm through the storm because we are "garrisoned" by the peace of God?

Note one final truth. There is a strange mixture of war and peace in the promise of our text. In fact, the Divine peace actually takes upon itself warlike functions here. The Divine peace is likened to a battalion of soldiers that is assigned to guide us through warfare and keep us safe. So the peace of God is not an escape mechanism. It is to be enjoyed in the midst of warfare. God's peace is militantly escorting us safely through the battlefield of life. And the man who has it still has to wage war with the world, the flesh, and the devil. Day by day he braces himself for the fight. But all through the fight, God's peace guards the door of his heart and mind so that the troubles on the outside need not come inside. The Old Testament says, "Keep your heart with all diligence, because out of it are the issues of life" (Proverbs 4:23). The New Testament tells us how to do it. Be careful for nothing; be prayerful about everything; be thankful for anything — and the peace of God will keep the citadel for you!

It is interesting to note two terms that are used in the text and context of our study. One is the term "the peace of God" in verse seven, the other is the term "the God of peace" in verse eight. Perhaps some reader does not have the peace of God and will never get it until he comes to know the God of peace. How do you know Him? Confess your sins directly to Him, and repent of them, trusting Him to help you. Remember that He loves you personally, so much, in fact, that He sent His Beloved Son to die on Calvary's Cross for you and your sins. But Jesus did not remain dead; He arose from the dead, revealing His victory over sin, and death, and hell. And He won this victory for you! He tells you in His Word that if you will totally trust Him and Him alone to save you, He will come into your life, forgive your sins, and give you the gift of eternal life. If you will receive Him into your heart today, He will receive you into His heaven when you leave this world. Trust Jesus today, then tell someone about your decision. Find a Bible-believing, Gospel-preaching church and begin to attend. And enroll in Christianity 101 today! You will find a lot of us in the same class!

Chapter 23

Something to Think About

"Finally, brethren, whatsoever things are true, whatsoever things are honest, whatsoever things are just, whatsoever things are pure, whatsoever things are lovely, whatsoever things are of good report; if there be any virtue, and if there be any praise, think on these things." (Philippians 4:8)

Dennis the Menace said to his friend Joey, "Thinking is when your mouth stays shut and your head keeps talking to itself." A pretty good definition of thinking—your head talks to itself. One of the biggest problems of an active human being is that he often does more uncontrolled vocal talking with his mouth than controlled virtual talking with his mind.

A well-known Scottish golfer recently came to the United States to play in one of the major golf tournaments here. He said some things before the tournament that alienated him from the American golf fan. A fellow Scotsman, a television commentator, later explained the player's problem in these words, "He sometimes sends his mind on vacation and leaves his mouth in charge." This is almost an occupational hazard with human beings.

Paul addresses the matter of the mind by letting us see that the *mind matters*, and it matters *much*. He summarizes Christian virtue and morality in a series of six marvelous terms—"true, honest, just, pure, lovely, of good report"—and urges his readers to "think on these things." One of the most instructive things we can do as we read such a passage is to consider the writer and the circumstance of writing. The writer is the Apostle Paul, and his circumstance at the time of writing is one of imprisonment. In fact, Paul's entire Christian life had been full of menace and turbulence. Every road he traveled as a believer seemed to be bristling with enmity and hostility. Paul's life reminds me of the man who facetiously said, "I had so much trouble that 911 called me to see if they could give any assistance."

But what a spirit, what an attitude, Paul had maintained! In spite of the innumerable difficulties he had faced, he had kept his spirit wholesome and unembittered. This lengthy sentence from his letter to the Philippian Christians rests upon the background of his life like a brilliant diamond on dark velvet. He is now an old man, with body bent and broken, and he is awaiting legal trial before an unsympathetic Roman judgment seat. He had every reason to lose hope and mental initiative. But instead, he is vibrant and alive, and is managing to grow old with an incredible amount of cheerfulness. He is rejoicing in "the glorious liberty of the children of God." He shares his secret with us in the counsel he gives to the Philippians in our text. Let's explore his counsel under two simple headings.

THE THINKING THAT CONTROLS HUMAN CREATURES

First, we will note that *human beings are controlled by thought.* Man has been defined as "the thinking animal." I agree, but I certainly don't want to be disrespectful to the other animals! And I don't want to leave the impression that I believe man is no more than a thinking animal.

The key word of verse eight is the word, "think." The key word of verse nine is the word, "do." These two verbs combine two of the greatest functions of the Christian life (indeed, of anyone's life), and they define areas in which most Christians are terribly weak. Practically, a Christian could be defined as one who thinks the best and does the best. And the order is consistent. A person's doing stems from his thinking just as an oak tree comes from an acorn. Marcus Aurelius is credited with the statement, "The happiness of your life depends upon the quality of your thoughts, therefore, guard them carefully. Your soul will be dyed the color of your inner thoughts." *Your perceptions will show in your practice. Prevailing attitudes become persistent actions.* This can be seen by stringing two related texts from the book of Proverbs on a common thread. Proverbs 4:23 says, "Keep your heart with all diligence, for out of it are the issues of life." Then, Proverbs 23:7 adds, "As a man thinks in his heart, so is he." One translation says, "Mind-heart" for the word translated in the KJV by "heart." Guard your mind-heart, wise old Solomon said, because out of your mind-heart your life is controlled. Thinking is an invisible activity, but it has very visible aftereffects. *The process is invisible, but the product is very, very visible.* This is true both positively and negatively. What does not mold the mind soon will not hold the heart or mobilize the feet, but what seizes the mind shapes the life.

Throughout Philippians chapter four, the Apostle Paul calls for several activities, both positive and negative, that require deliberate mental exertion. In verse four, he commands us to *"rejoice."* Anyone who has ever tried to "rejoice evermore" has discovered that this is simply not possible without a regular tuning of the mind.

In verse six, Paul commands us to *"be anxious for nothing,"* or, "don't worry about anything." I heard of a man who was a chronic worry-wart, an apparently incurable worrier. One day, however, a friend met him on the street and he was sauntering along indifferently, whistling a happy tune. Sensing a great difference in him, the friend asked, "Well, what has gotten into you? You are not your usual serious self." "Oh, I went to see a psychiatrist, and he cured me of my worrying." "Really! He must be a wonderful psychiatrist." "Oh, he is!" "How did he cure you of worrying?" "He told me just to surrender all of my worries to him and he would take care of them." "Well, it surely seems to be working. And how much did he charge you for his services?" "A thousand dollars an hour." "A thousand dollars an hour! How are you going to pay it?" The happy man replied, "That's his worry!" Worry is a corrosive habit that will only be corrected by an overhauling of the mind.

Also in verse six, Paul counsels a course of *"prayer and supplication with thanksgiving."* These three activities begin with mental premises. Isolate the word "thanksgiving" for a moment. There is only one letter's difference between the word "think" and the word "thank." Everyone who thinks consistently with his mind (that is, in a manner that is *consistent with truth*) must thank continually from his heart.

Looking past verse eight in Philippians chapter four, you can easily see several exercises that call for diligent and disciplined use of the mind. The three great "victory statements" in verses 12, 13, and 19 would be impractical and impossible without control of the mind. To *"know both how to be abased, and how to abound,"* to be able to say *"I can do all things through Christ who strengthens me,"* and to declare that *"My God shall supply all your need according to His riches in glory by Christ Jesus"* will sound unreal to anyone who has not cultivated a Christian mind. But to the person with such a mind, these statements describe delightful realities and continual aspirations of his life.

Is the cultivation and control of the mind a major matter or a minor matter? The well-known Christian apologist Cornelius Van Til built his entire Christian philosophy on this premise: A person's presuppositions determine everything for that person. Further, Van Til said that unless one presupposes that God has given truth, there is no way to be sure of anything. For Van Til, only the assumption that God is sovereign and has revealed the truth in the Bible (His Word) will save humanity from the otherwise totally confusing voices of human reason. Another Christian theologian, Frances Schaeffer, echoed the same premises in his book, *Escape From Reason*.

Please read the last paragraph again, noting the "mental words" in it: "apologist, philosophy, premise, presuppositions, assumptions, truth, confusion, reason." You see, all of life is determined by the mind. The mind is the "control panel" that determines the direction, the dynamic and the destination of each human being. Furthermore, the human mind will be controlled either by *human reason* or by *Divine revelation*.

Even the text is admittedly based on a presupposition: There is a category in human life that is marked by "excellence" (a category that has only one dimension—perfection), and there are many things that are "worthy of praise." Read verse eight once more and see the emphasis on these two things: "If there is any excellence and if anything worthy of praise." It must be noted that, according to Scripture, these excellent and praiseworthy things are found only in and through Jesus Christ and His Gospel.

The Bible is a reflection of these foundational premises: (1) There is *objective* truth (truth that exists independently of us, whether or not we know it, accept it, or approve or disapprove of it); (2) This truth is *absolute* (unchanging, totally demanding, and totally determinative); and (3) This truth is *universal* (it is true for everyone without exception, exemption or exclusion). A human being may reject these premises with his God-given mind, but he cannot escape the consequences of this rejection. When a person dances, he must pay the fiddler. If he is at the wrong dance, he will finally collapse in eternal despair. But if he is at the right dance, Someone has already sponsored it for him, and he will enjoy it forever! Incidentally, this analogy is based on the great debate that has been carried on by scientists, philosophers and theologians for time immemorial, *Is life Chance or Dance?* That is, is life the result of random accident, or is it carefully orchestrated and symphonized by a Divine Conductor?

So it is absolutely imperative that every serious Christian develop the best thoughts, attitudes and motives, the things that will govern his entire life. Someone stated it this way: "We are not what we think we are. Rather, what we *think*, we *are*." *We are what we think!* There is no such thing as a cozy corner where you and I can go to think our own thoughts as we want to think them so that no one else will know. If we think ourselves to be humble, gifted, charming people, we will go right out of our "cozy corner" and act superior, haughty and cold. If we think critical thoughts of someone while we are in our "corner," we will leave it to find our speech necessarily dripping with verbal venom. If we think lustful thoughts, we will march out of our corner to enact lustful deeds. We gradually become what our thinking conditions us to be. A Christian author named Harry Blamires wrote a book entitled *The Christian Mind*. It is the responsibility of every believer in Christ to maintain a Christian mind.

David prayed for such a mind when he said, "Let the words of my mouth, and *the meditation of my heart* (my heart-mind), be acceptable in Thy sight, O Lord, my strength and my redeemer" (Psalm 19:14). The prophet Isaiah went to the end of the line in the other direction, pointing out what we can expect if we continue to cultivate Godless, impure minds. Isaiah quotes God as saying, "I also will choose their delusions, and will bring their fears upon them; because when I called, none did answer; when I spake, they did not hear: but they did evil before my eyes, and chose that in which I delighted not" (Isaiah 66:4). If I allow my God-given mind to maintain evil or untrue thoughts, God will see to it that certain fears and delusions will be the inevitable final consequences of my choosing the evil thoughts and refusing the Christian thoughts. But in a world that seeks to bury us in unChristian thoughts, how is this refusing of the evil and the choosing of the good to be done?

THE THINGS ON WHICH CHRISTIANS ARE TO CONCENTRATE

There are *certain large categories of thought on which Christians are to concentrate.* "Think on these things," Paul commanded his readers. The word translated "think" is not the usual word that is used for thinking. It is the word *logizomai*, which means to "reckon," or "calculate," or "consider." The word "reckon" means to count something as true and act upon it. The word "calculate" describes what a builder does when he takes careful measurements before attempting to build. One paraphrase says, "Take account of these things with a view to committing yourselves to them." The New American Standard Version of the New Testament captures the basic meaning of the phrase by this translation, "Let your mind dwell on these things." This is the Scriptural version of positive thinking.

The six virtues that are mentioned in the text are to be practiced as well as praised. One young Sunday School boy said, "The Bible begins with Genesis and ends with Revolutions," and, while technically inaccurate, his statement was unwittingly true. *What personal, moral, and social revolutions would occur if Christians were to consistently* and *happily obey this command!* When John Wesley began to issue the rules or "methods" that created the Methodist Church, some of his followers began to question and alter some of the rules. Wesley then established another rule: *"These rules are to be minded, not mended."* We must "mind" the matters of the mind without mending them if we would have a Christian mind.

The word translated "think" is a present imperative verb. The imperative means that this is an absolute, unqualified command, and the present tense means that our thoughts are to constantly move in the six areas specified in this verse. When the two verb-facets, the present tense and the imperative mood, are combined together, *they call for a total commitment to a nonstop way of thinking, and for a deliberate discrimination which rejects everything unworthy of such thinking.* Furthermore, the word *logizomai* is based on the Greek word logos, which is the word from which we derive our English word, "logic." So Paul is commanding believers to let Christian thought be the logic of their lives.

Random thinking is perhaps the easiest thing human beings ever do, but *right thinking* is perhaps the *hardest thing* we ever do. Christians, of all people, ought to be great thinkers, and they should pay the price to be right thinkers. This is true because: (1) Christians worship God, and He is the Creative Thinker (!) who made this vast universe; (2) Christians follow Jesus Christ as His "disciples," a word which basically means "student," or "pupil," or "learner," and includes the idea that Christ Himself had a clear and keen mind; and (3) Christians are members of an historic fellowship called the "Church," which has always encouraged learning. *No person can be a serious and practicing Christian (a "real" Christian, we say) without the developing and disciplined use of the mind.*

It was author Christopher Morley who coined the word "inscape." Your landscape is what you see outside yourself, your external world. Your *inscape* is what you see with your inner eye, the eye that stimulates and confines your thoughts. Paul indicates in our text that a Christian's inscape should be occupied with six expansive categories of thought. We will look briefly at each one.

"Whatsoever things are *true* ... think on these things." The first category in the list is the most important. Truth is the first thing that should occupy a Christian's mind. *Until we have made friends with truth, we have no lasting friends.* The word translated "true" is *alethe*, which means that which is factually true in contrast to that which is false. All truth is God's truth, even when it is artificially divided into "secular" and "sacred." The source of truth is God the Father (John 3:33), God the Son (John 14:6), and God the Holy Spirit (John 14:17). Thus, it has no falsehood, deceit, or impurity in it. J. H. Jowett made this distinction: "Truth in a police court is correspondence with fact. Truth in the New Testament is *correspondence with God*." So a Christian should anchor his life to God's revealed truth and let it be the touchstone of his thoughts and his life.

"Whatsoever things are *honorable* ... think on these things." The Greek word is *semnos*, which means "worthy of respect." Everyone knows the comic lament of Rodney Dangerfield, "I don't get no respect." The whole point is that he doesn't deserve respect. Life has its own built-in assessments. Not being built upon Divine truth, one's life simply cannot finally be "honorable." The Christian, on the other hand, should build his life around that which is worthy of respect. Tennyson said of King Arthur and Sir Launcelot, "These two were the most noble-mannered men of all; For manners are not idle, but the fruit of loyal nature and of noble mind." Paul indicates that if the mind of Christ is in us, we will be controlled by things that are worthy of reverence. We will be "noble-mannered" people, with "noble mind and loyal nature."

"Whatsoever things are *just* ... think on these things." The word is *dikaios*, which also means "righteous," something that has the stamp of God upon it because only God can produce righteousness. It refers to that which corresponds to the divine standard. The believer has been made righteous, or right with God, through faith in Jesus Christ. His life has been rightly adjusted to his Maker, and he should think on things that satisfy and reflect the standards of the God who has saved him. He should think about that which is right, not that which is wrong. Again, the foundation for this righteousness is God's truth.

"Whatsoever things are *pure* ... think on these things." Remember that the characteristic at the head of the list is the most important. If a person is truly anchored to that which is true in his thoughts and his life, the other characteristics will show up in his life. Remember, too, that many of Paul's readers had only recently been saved from impurity and immorality. They had worshiped in a religion that regularly featured activity with temple prostitutes. But captured by truth, they were now asked to commit their thinking to things that were morally stainless, blameless, and unblemished. The word is *hagnos*, which is the root word for "holy." The Christian should set his goal to think on holy things.

"Whatsoever things are *lovely* ... think on these things." Here the word is *prosphile*, which means "beautiful, admirable, attractive, agreeable, and pleasing." The Christian goal is winsomeness and attractiveness. Every believer should have a winsome lifestyle of attractive happiness which will be magnetic to everyone around him. The word Paul used has to do with relationships, and again we face the necessity to develop winsome relational skills when dealing with other people. Christians are to think on that which fosters harmony rather than on that which causes strife. When I am related to truth (characteristic number one in the list), people become very, very important to me, and relationships are crucial. A word of caution is due at this point: If one's lifestyle is not based solidly upon Divine truth, any magnetism that he exerts will be merely fleshly magnetism, sterile of God's endorsement, and will attract people to Satan's camp (where he himself lives). What a contrast to a "lovely" life!

"Whatsoever things are of *good report* ... think on these things." The word here is *euphemos*. Drs. Moulton and Milligan in their Greek lexicon suggest that this word "signifies the delicacy which guards the lips." In other words, our thoughts should give rise to expressions of the lips that would affirm other people and not scandalize them, and we should seek a lifestyle for ourselves that would easily allow others to give a good report of us. Is the report that people give of you when they spontaneously think and talk about you a truly "good" report morally and spiritually? Or is an automatic moral frown raised on Christian brows when they think of you? The Psalmist prayed, "Set a watch, O Lord, before my mouth; keep the door of my lips" (Psalm 141:3). Here, the guard is placed over the mind as well, so that both the mind and the mouth are dominated by "things of good report." Again, remember that no genuine "good report" can be given that is not based on God's revealed truth. "Whatever things are true" is the monitor that heads the list.

"Since there is a category labeled 'excellence,' and since there are praiseworthy things, *think on these things*." William Hendriksen said, "Anything at all that is a matter of moral and spiritual excellence, so that it is the proper object of praise, is the right pasture for the Christian mind to graze in. Nothing that is of a contrary nature is the right food for his thoughts." J. H. Jowett wrote, "This is the vast and authorized circle for our mental hospitality. Therefore, let us often go abroad in our territory on journeys of exploration. Everywhere our eyes will be surprised by gracious discoveries, and by fastening our minds upon these things, we shall be 'children of light.'"

Before I conclude this chapter, let me make a few general suggestions about the training of your thoughts in order to develop a Christian mind. Then I will close with a few practical suggestions. If you are to develop a truly Christian mind, *a special determination and a spiritual discrimination are necessary.* If your mind is allowed to drift, it will invariably drift toward moral and spiritual shipwreck.

One day as a mother was scraping and peeling the vegetables for a salad, her daughter came through the kitchen holding a book which she was reading. The mother's inquiry disclosed that the book was a piece of filthy fiction. As the girl reacted against her mother's kind and loving suggestion that she should not be reading such books, suddenly she saw her mother pick up a handful of discarded vegetable scraps and throw them into the salad. In a startled voice the girl cried, "Mother, you are putting the garbage in the salad!" "Yes," her mother replied calmly, "I know, but I thought that if you did not mind garbage in your mind and head, you certainly would not mind a little in your stomach!" Martin Luther was right when he said, "You may not be able to prevent birds from flying over your head, but you can keep them from building a nest in your hair." Today, because of the bombardment of our minds with a barrage of "filthy flak," we must be very careful to steadily fill our minds with the best, and to filter out the bad.

A Christian mind will not just "happen" without effort and determination. The new birth alone will never produce a Christian mind, any more than mere physical birth without growth, learning and training will yield a philosopher. A Christian mind, like any other mind, is made of thoughts, and the development of a Christian mind requires the focus of those thoughts on Christian things.

Then, *steady spiritual discipline* is necessary. Anyone who aspires to a Christian mind must train his mind by regular practice to find delight in the broad and pleasing categories Paul specified in our text. But how do we practice such a discipline? How do we develop such a mind? Let me be very practical as I conclude this study. The final suggestions will sound so simple and earthy, but they are urgent.

Every Christian *should maximize the occasions when he hears the proclamation of God's truth* (the first characteristic in the list). Jesus said it in three crucial mandates: "Be careful that you hear;" "be careful what you hear;" and "be careful how you hear." Your quest for a Christian mind will begin and end with the intake of God's truth. Prepare your heart in advance for the truth God entrusts to you through sermons, Bible study lessons and individual quiet times, determining to hear God's voice and obey His instructions. Also, discipline yourself to always take notes on the truths received so that you can retain them and relay them on to others.

Then, every Christian *should maintain a regular Christian reading program*—even at the cost of other leisure activities (such as watching television, which today might be better labeled "lust" than "leisure"). Hardly any other activity has changed my life over nearly fifty years of being a Christian like the selective reading of Christian books. Charles Spurgeon, the great British preacher, read *Pilgrim's Progress* over one hundred times, or twice a year, and this was only the tiniest part of his reading. Thomas de Quincey said, "All great literature becomes a Jacob's ladder from earth to mysterious altitudes above the earth." The alternative, which is a fairly good picture of the intellectual climate of most Americans today, was pictured in the child's classic, *The Adventures of Pinocchio*. The puppet Pinocchio sought out (and found) a leisure land where no discipline was practiced. He found that there were no schools, no teachers, no books in this strange land. Pinocchio declared that a land without books where nobody studies "is a delightful land. The days are spent in play and amusement from morning 'til night, day after day." However, Pinocchio finally realizes (and so shall we) that the place is "a land of blockheads and donkeys." The United Negro College Fund commercial that says "a mind is too valuable a thing to waste" should be heard and heeded by every responsible human being. And a Christian should aspire to far higher goals than merely the rescue of his mind from waste.

Many statues have been made throughout human history to represent man. Some have shown him as the worker with his hammer, hoe, or shovel in his hand. Others have portrayed him as the warrior, dressed in his armor and ready for battle. Still others have pictured him as the athlete — running, leaping, throwing the discus, slam-dunking a basketball, striking a tennis ball or a golf ball, side-stepping a tackler, or holding a trophy as he celebrates a victory. But one of the most remarkable of all statues representing man is a world-renowned statue in which a man is shown who is not engaged in any obvious physical activity; not equipped with any kind of armor; not holding any sort of implement. He is just sitting there with his elbow propped on his knee and his chin resting in his cupped hand, pondering, wondering, meditating, dreaming—just thinking. The name of that statue by the famous French sculptor, Auguste Rodin, is *Le Penseur*, "The Thinker." Christians should hold this sculpted masterpiece as a living ideal in their lives, with a plaque underneath providing the Christian content: "Finally, brethren, whatever is true, whatever is honorable, whatever is right, whatever is pure, whatever is lovely, whatever is of good repute, since there is a category called 'excellence' and since there are many things worthy of praise, let your mind dwell on these things." May it be so with each of us, for the glory of God, for our own eternal welfare, and for the eternal good of our fellow men.

Chapter 24

The Secret of Serenity

"But I rejoiced in the Lord greatly, that now at the last your care of me hath flourished again; wherein ye were also careful, but ye lacked opportunity. Not that I speak in respect of want: for I have learned, in whatsoever state I am, therewith to be content. I know both how to be abased, and I know how to abound: everywhere and in all things I am instructed both to be full and to be hungry, both to abound and to suffer need. I can do all things through Christ which strengtheneth me." (Phlippians 4:10-13)

    The entire countenance of civilized society was changed by the horrible and heartless events of September 11, 2001. Launching clearly from a base of radical religion which spawns extreme violence, and apparently believing their cause to be perfectly right, a group of men bent on producing as much destruction, distress, havoc and disarray as possible in the United States followed a diabolical scheme to attack our society at its governing and economic centers. Their success has been chronicled on all major news networks nearly every minute since the attacks. Many years ago, Bishop Hall said, "For every bad, there is a worse; when a man breaks his leg, let him be thankful it was not his neck." As horrendous as the destruction was, it certainly could have been worse. It seems that the terrorists had other targets in mind, but were thwarted by both the heroism of individuals who were circumstantially included in their plans, and by circumstances that were not favorable to their efforts. Furthermore, we are now being firmly warned by officials in our national government that there may be other terrorist attacks of varying kinds.

What is a Christian to think during such times? How is he to react? What is he to do? Personally, I am not at all surprised by the human depravity that is revealed in such actions, or at the inhumanity that they disclose. Human history is replete with such accounts. A long time ago, Alexander Pope spoke ominously of "man's inhumanity to man," and every generation seems to outdo all others in revealing it. My amazement at the recent events is centered in the "mix" of religion, fanaticism, suicide for inhuman (and religious) purposes, the attempt to cover all of this under a guise of "faith" and "martyrdom," and the wholesale enlistment of men out of a society to do this. Still, the question presses upon us, How should a Christian respond? Two things are obvious: (1) A Christian must never abandon love as his mode of operation, even to loving our enemies, and praying for them (read Matthew 5:44 again, and carefully). Yes, we must lovingly pray for any and all of those whose intent toward us is destructive. (2) A Christian must never abandon his firm faith in God and the Gospel. But it is precisely at these points that we tend to struggle the most.

Recently, I found this paragraph in a book by Mike Mason: "During a time of particular spiritual oppression, when I could not seem to shake the sense that God was implacably disappointed in me, I was walking by the ocean one morning when I spied a child's valentine lying in the sand. The message read, 'You're okay with me, Valentine.' I took it home and showed it to my wife, who promptly wrote on it, 'To Mike / Love, God.' Suddenly, the incredible truth came home to me again, and it came with such force that it was as if I had never heard it before. *Isn't it funny how a person can be a Christian and not really know the Gospel?* Isn't it strange how Christ can live inside us without our really enjoying Him? This Gospel, it turns out, is not only good news—it is much better news that any of us has yet imagined." (The italics in this paragraph are mine, not the author's) However, this "mix" of Gospel, love and faith does not deliver us from the realism of a world in which deeds such as the September 11 events can occur.

In recent years Christians in the United States have been reminded again of the kind of enemy we face and the kind of weapons which must be used to defeat that enemy. The Christian community must place itself on "red alert" at such times, not so much an alert to danger as an alert to opportunity. The events of 9/11 both prove the need for world evangelism by Christians, and present an incredible opportunity to share the Gospel when men's hearts are alert, sensitive and questioning. Not the least of the opportunities to be capitalized at present is the opportunity to openly compare Christianity and religion. The television newscasters have reported a large increase among booksellers in sales of books about Islam, the Koran, prophecy, the Bible, and faith. What a time to immediately explore comparative world-views and comparative world religions. Christianity has absolutely nothing to fear from exposure of its total truth on an open market of ideas. *A Gospel that highlights a resurrection and features a risen Savior cannot lose in an open market—unless its adherents fail to take it into that market!* Since Islam is the religion that is most in the news, Islam must be confronted as to the real nature of its views about tolerance, violence, God, man. It must be asked about its practical interpretation of such terms as "jihad," or "holy war," and how the enemy is recognized for the perpetration of such war. *In western society, Islam is free to put its ideas on the open market for consideration, but in Islamic societies, no such freedom is granted to Christians and others.* Why? A faith that is true should be confident enough to face down all comers. Of course, "defending and advancing God's truth" is the avowed reason, but this is often only a guise to veil intolerance and fanaticism.

In a very soft and encouraging letter which I received by e-mail from a dear Hispanic brother just after the attacks upon New York and Washington, these "hard" words were included: "This is a time for many people to understand that all religions that are contrary to Jesus Christ are vicious and harmful to mankind, all philosophies that do not appreciate the Gospel as the message from God are poisonous and only feed the anger and violence of human hearts. Religion without Christ tends to make horrible fanatics, not redeemed people. Religion without Christ only brings death." I might add that *this is also true of those who only have the "christian religion" without a relationship with God through Jesus Christ.* We often call them "nominal Christians," but they are simply lost people who have accepted some "christian" ideas and standards without being born again. They may be in church every Sunday, but each of them is only old Adam in Sunday clothes! This is a serious charge, and many over-tolerant people will object to it. But the charge is still true. I want to say again that my Hispanic brother's letter was long, warm, and encouraging, and that the above quotation formed only a tiny part of his letter. Our Christian faith requires us to find the balance between truly loving our enemies and praying for those who treat us spitefully (no easy ethic!), and seeking true and realistic justice in society (again, an ethic that is humanly impossible).

Now is a time to study Philippians, a book that is especially timely for our lives today. The theme of Philippians is contentment. More specifically, it is contentment in spite of evil circumstances. Is that timely enough? What a field of study and application is presented in the four verses that comprise the text. Surely Paul could not have known how applicable his statements would be in a far-away society two thousand years after they were written, but the Holy Spirit knew! And the Holy Spirit just as easily had us in mind as He had Paul in mind. Through the pen of an Apostle imprisoned in a Roman jail, He addressed a nation imprisoned behind the less definable walls of shock, fear, uncertainty, insecurity, and anger. I am grateful for Paul's words, and I ask you to join me in a simple examination of them.

THE CONCEPT OF CONTENTMENT

First, we must give careful attention to the *concept of contentment*, and we must be certain that we understand the Biblical view.

Just what is contentment, anyway? How is it to be defined and described? This is very important, else several subtle substitutes be confused for contentment.

It may be helpful in delivering us from wrong ideas about the Christian view of contentment by beginning negatively. It is important to know what contentment is not, as well as to know what it is.

Contentment is not fatalism, or the acceptance of evil with a shrug of helpless resignation. In no case is contentment to be confused with mere resignation. And contentment is not complacency. In the preceding chapter (3:12-14), Paul said that he was not satisfied with his present level of maturity and accomplishment as a Christian, but was in hot pursuit of the Christian ideal. Neither is contentment the enemy of proper ambition. The desire and effort to improve one's life for himself and others are not opposed to contentment. Contentment is not to be confused with an innocent and idyllic "polyanna" philosophy of life, which is innocently blind to all adversity, or a "candide" view that "this is the best of all possible worlds," and nothing can be done or should be done to try to improve it. Contentment is not indifference to evil circumstances. Contentment is not carelessness, nor is it self-satisfaction. Furthermore, it is not a cop-out to avoid radical responsibility. Indeed, there is no true contentment until the individual has squarely faced and overcome every circumstance of his life. A contented person is not the helpless victim of circumstances, but the victor over any circumstance of his life. Furthermore, he is seriously and aggressively offering his victory in Christ to others.

When the Speaker of the English House of Lords puts a question to that body, instead of saying, "All in favor of the motion, let it be known by saying, 'Aye,' he says, "All that favor, let it be known by saying, 'Content.' This is a proper acknowledgment that contentment is not a passive but an active virtue. Paul had learned to give an honest and solid vote of approval to every experience of his life. This does not mean that he recognized every circumstance as good in itself, but rather that it had been permitted by a good God who would use it for good in his life. One wise man echoed this idea when he said that a victorious man can "meet with Triumph and Disaster, And treat those two imposters just the same."

Paul's words could be accurately paraphrased like this, "I have that within me that is greater than all circumstances. Rather, I have One in me Who has conquered all circumstances, and stands ready to enforce His victory in me." Does not the Bible say, "You are of God, little children, and have overcome them, because *greater is He that is in you than he that is in the world*"? (I John 4:4) So contentment is not based on the circumstances of the outward man, but on the content of the inward man.

When Paul said, "I have learned in every circumstance to be content," the word translated "content" is the Greek word *autarkia*. This is a compound Greek word which means "self-sufficient." Again, great caution must be exercised in understanding this word. The term "self-sufficient" may be properly used by a Christian in a good way or in a bad way. In the bad sense, the word "self-sufficient" means independent and self-centered. This independence is the very essence of sin. In the good sense, the word means "self-contained." The word is used to describe an individual who truly has all the resources he really needs within himself. But this is true only of a Christian. When Jesus Christ lives in a person, as He does in every Christian, that person certainly has all the resources he really needs for victory in life, in death, and in eternity. Thus, he is also independent, but this independence is the very essence of faith.

I was raised in the state of Arkansas. Many times when I was a young boy and a young man, I heard the boast of state leaders that Arkansas was "the only state in the United States that could be completely self-containing." That is, if the borders were closed, the state could easily survive by its own resources, because they are sufficient. That is reasonably what Paul means by the word translated "content." Remember the term, "self-containing." It is evident that Paul did not exclude God or His providence from his formula for contentment. He said elsewhere, "Not as if we were sufficient of ourselves, but our sufficiency is of God." Every Christian should be able to draw on the resources of Christ within him so that he is victoriously "self-containing." This is the meaning of Paul's word.

Let me conclude this first point by giving a definition of Christian contentment. Christian contentment is the regular maintenance of positive peace in any circumstance of life. It is the ability to happily accept either adversity or prosperity with spiritual serenity. It is the ability to "do all things" called for in any and all situations "through Christ who keeps on infusing me with His strength" (Philippians 4:13).

THE CLASSROOM OF CONTENTMENT

Second, we need to look into *the classroom* where Paul learned contentment. In verses 11 and 12, he said, "I have learned, in whatsoever state I am, therewith to be content. I know both how to be abased, and I know how to abound: everywhere and in all things I am instructed both to be full and to be hungry, both to abound and to suffer need." What a magnificent statement! And it becomes even bigger with the understanding of the words Paul used. Note the words, "I have learned," and "I am instructed." These are classroom words. The word translated "instructed" is *mueo*, which meant "to be initiated into a secret." This is the word that is used for the induction process into the mystery religions of Paul's day, or might be used for induction into a secret order today. What does this mean? Is Christianity like Freemasonry, which has secrets which are divulged only to the inductees? Well, yes and no. Christianity does contain secrets, and unhappily, they are often well-kept secrets. However, it does not harbor secrets intentionally, as Freemasonry does. It does not intend to "keep" secrets, but it has many things within it that are secrets in the sense that very few learn them.

Reach for a dictionary and look up the word *esoteric*. This is a very meaningful word, though not commonly used. The word means "understood by only a select group; belonging only to a select number; private, secret, confidential; intended to be communicated only to the initiated." Christianity is esoteric in this sense:

it is understood and experienced only by insiders, only by those who are initiated into its life and privileges by a spiritual birth and a spiritual walk. *It is like the stain-glass window of a cathedral at noonday. The outsider will not see or appreciate its content, but the insider will experience its full radiance and glory.* It is a matter of naivete to take an outsider's opinion about Christianity as authoritative. He simply cannot know what he is taking about, and his presumption is pathetic. But the spiritual Christian is party to all the truths that are "secrets" to outsiders.

The offer of the Gospel is made to all, but only those wise enough to respond to Christ on His terms will see or experience the full glory of it. Contentment is one such truth, one such "experience," one such glorious reality. Only those who go "far enough up and in" will know this secret. Only those who know the *blood-mark* of Christ's mighty redemption, the *birth-mark* of Christ's mighty salvation, and the *bond-mark* of His magnificent service, can know real contentment. And even with those "esoteric" qualifications, this lesson must be learned over a slow and painful course. No one acquires contentment in a quantum leap. Each believer must serve his apprenticeship in the school of Christ if he is to learn the lesson of contentment.

Paul said, "I have learned how to be abased and how to abound." His contentment had been extended to every circumstance of his life. Now, it is easy for us to sit in our relative ease and comfort, or in only moderate difficulty, and shrug our shoulders at Paul's statement. But one cannot read the book of Acts without knowing that Paul lived almost without relief in a climate of crisis. If you want a summary, ready II Corinthians 11:23-28. I am personally embarrassed when I read this "catalogue of crises" from Paul's pen. It was in this climate, in this context, in this *classroom*, that Paul was initiated into the secret of contentment.

He said, "I know how to be abased." Only a person ignorant of Paul's life would challenge this declaration. He was knocked down again and again to the basement of life, and while at the bottom, he learned the invincibility of Christian contentment.

He also said, "I know how to abound," and this lesson may be even more difficult to learn than the other. One Sunday morning years ago in First Baptist Church of Dallas, Texas, Dr. George Truett, the pastor, received a note from a church leader while seated in the pastor's chair and waiting to preach. When he rose to preach, he made this announcement: "We need to pause for special prayer for a member who has come to sudden crisis in his life." Then he mentioned the member's name and prayed for him. At the end of the service, Dr. Truett said, "I think I neglected to mention the nature of our brother's new crisis. A rich relative in his family has died, and he has inherited a fortune. *This may prove to be the hardest crisis he will face in his lifetime.*" Friends, it is harder to carry a full cup than an empty one. Our society may be the most restless society in history, yet we are the most affluent people the world has ever known.

The Bible presents the Christian ideal in these words: "Let your lifestyle be without covetousness; and be content with such things as you have: for He hath said, I will never leave thee, nor forsake thee. So that we may boldly say, The Lord is my helper, and *I will not fear what man shall do unto me*" (Hebrews 13:5). Note that man may do many things to me, adverse things, deadly things, diabolical things, even to taking my life, but I still need not fear, because nothing shall separate from the love of God which is manifested to me through Jesus Christ my Lord (Romans 8:37-39). As a Christian, I am forever enveloped in the redemptive love of Christ. Note also the clear order expressed in Hebrews 13:5: "He hath said" . . . "so that we may boldly say." When our lives and lips echo the clear truth of God's revealed Word, we will have contentment!

While studying for this message, I came across a great list of truths in a sermon on contentment preached by the late great London pastor, Dr. D. Martyn Lloyd-Jones. He calls them steps in Paul's logic as he builds his argument about Christian contentment. Here is the list: "(1) God is concerned about me as my Father, and nothing happens to me apart from God. Even the very hairs of my head are all numbered. I must never forget that. (2) God's will and God's ways are a great mystery, but I know that whatever He wills or permits is of necessity for my good. (3) Every situation in life is the unfolding of some manifestation of God's love and goodness. Therefore my business is to look for this peculiar manifestation of God's goodness and kindness and to *be prepared for surprises* (italics mine) and blessings because 'His ways are not my ways, neither His thoughts my thoughts'. (4) I must regard circumstances and conditions, not in and of themselves, therefore, but as a part of God's dealings with me in the work of perfecting my soul and bringing me to final perfection. (5) Whatever my conditions may be at this present moment they are only temporary, they are only passing, and they can never rob me of the joy and the glory that ultimately await me in Christ." We need to rehearse this list in our minds and hearts until these truths become "first nature" to us.

All of us need to select a seat in Christ's classroom, and ask Him to teach us these lessons which lead to contentment.

THE COMPONENTS OF CONTENTMENT

Finally, we will examine some of the *components* of contentment. What are the working parts of contentment? Though there are many, I would mention just two.

The first component of Christian contentment is *a solid doctrinal foundation*. Now, this will disturb the mentally lazy person, the person who is slouchy and indifferent in his thinking. But that person will also remain without true contentment. He will not know his loss or his deficiency until some shock interrupts his life either personally, domestically, socially or nationally—such as the recent attacks on the United States. Then he will discover that he "failed to thatch his roof before the storm came." What an advantage the studious and spiritual Christian has in situations like that! And it is definitely time to check the kind of "thatching" that you have done on "your roof," because it looks like some devastating storms may be coming!

But what doctrine is most vital in securing Christian contentment? This doctrine—*the sovereignty of God*. And the attending doctrine—*the Lordship of Christ*. You see, we hold these doctrines because they represent eternal bedrock reality. The person who truly knows that God is in control of his life and of his world, and that Jesus is absolute Lord, may be contented in any circumstance. When a Christian believes that his condition, whatever it is, is determined by God, or at least is permitted by Him according to His pleasure, then that Christian can learn to capitalize adversity for his own advantage, for the good of others, and for God's glory. He knows that all things are ordered wisely and kindly by a heavenly Father. He knows that his Father is working everything together for good, though the good may not yet be seen. He knows that the present threatening circumstance will finally work for him and others "an exceeding and eternal weight of glory," and that he cannot finally lose in any situation.

One of the greatest hymns ever written is entitled, "How Firm a Foundation." Many who sing it never pause to meditate on its words and thus miss the blessing of those words. Furthermore, most hymnals include only four stanzas, but the original song had five. If we could appreciate the meaning of the original third stanza, we could better know "how to be abased," or how to face less-than-desirable circumstances in our lives. Here is the original third stanza, followed by the more familiar fourth stanza. I have also supplied italics to the words which speak of our "secret":

When through the deep waters I call thee to go,
The rivers of woe shall not thee overflow;
For I will be with thee thy troubles to bless,
And sanctify to thee thy deepest distress.
When through fiery trials thy pathway shall lie,
My grace, all-sufficient, shall be thy supply;
The flame shall not hurt thee; I only design
Thy dross to consume, and thy gold to refine.

I must be very careful to say that the sentiments stated in these words of the great hymn apply only to Christians. God addresses non-Christians with a different message.

The following paragraphs were written shortly after the "horrible events" of the infamous date 9/11 of recent American history. Because of the truths in these paragraphs, I have decided to include them in this volume as originally written:

With regard to the horrible events on and since 9/11, let me bluntly say that they were orchestrated by God (and frankly, it makes little difference to me whether you say they were "caused" or only "permitted" by Him), that they were unquestionably necessary in His Providence (and the most likely reason was to clearly and firmly address this nation) for the highest good at the least loss, and that He intends this nation to make a radical adjustment to Him at this time. The adjustment called for includes radical repentance of personal and national sin and the practice of a radical and happy daily walk with Him on a personal basis. To the person without Christ, these events should alert him to repent of his sins and trust Jesus Christ as his own personal Savior and Lord, and thus to begin the same kind of contented and happy walk with Christ that all Christians are to have.

Since I have mentioned the recent New York/Washington terrorist acts in this message, someone will voice the age-old protest, "Then, if God is really sovereign, why did He allow these things? Why didn't He prevent them?" This is, in effect, a request for God to totally eradicate evil from the world. But there are many, many implications of this request which we probably are not willing to face. You see, if you are asking for a total eradication of evil from the world, you are dictating something about yourself first. You are, in effect, asking for a total eradication of yourself! After all, are you not a sinner?

Let me answer the protest with an illustration that was shared by Dr. Kenneth Foreman, professor of doctrinal theology at Louisville Presbyterian Theological Seminary: "Imagine two horsemen.

One sits astride a horse, every movement of which he initiates and controls absolutely. The horse does not move a fraction of an inch in any part unless the rider decides it shall so move and sees to it that the movement is made. Here we see absolute control. The other rider sits on another horse. This horse makes various movements which the rider does not command or initiate. But the rider is still fully in control. The first horse is a hobbyhorse; the second is a spirited five-gaited show horse. But which is the better horseman? The boy operating his mechanical horse in the corner drugstore, or the prize-winning rider at the horse show? Is it actually more to God's credit that He shall ride His universe like a hobbyhorse, or like something alive with intelligence and spirit?" The answer surely seems to be self-evident to me. The ingredients of practical risk, real though limited human freedom (within prescribed limits sovereignly determined by God), and human responsibility, must be admitted in order to honor Scripture and see reality.

You see, we must hold a high view of God's perfect sovereignty, but we do not take away the modified self-determining freedoms which the Bible gives to man in order to hold that view. If those freedoms are not intact, the idea of cultivating contentment is a vain idea. But Paul clearly pictured those freedoms when he spoke of learning the lesson of contentment and being instructed in Christ's classroom of life.

The other component of contentment I would mention is a *strong devotional faith*. This, too, can be easily misunderstood. The word "devotional" is often taken to mean quiet and peaceful. But your devotional life is your total life of commitment to Jesus Christ, whether it occurs in the your living room, your prayer closet or in the middle of a howling mob.

Any true devotional faith has a negative side and a positive side to it. Negatively, it will mean the elimination of certain things from your life. Author Sue Bender dismissed a lot of contentment-killers from her life when she explained her personal victory as a Christian in these words: "Contentment came from giving up wishing I was someone else, or somewhere else, or doing something else." You see, all factors that oppose contentment must be weeded out of your character if you are to be truly contented. There are some things that are natural to sinners that must not be spared. One is pride—the pride of thinking that I am really a good person (against all the contrary evidence), or that nothing is too good for me, or that I am too good to be subjected to evil circumstances. Another is self-preference, a subtle but deadly attitude which is natural to sinners. Jesus solves this problem by commanding us to love our neighbors as ourselves. Another contentment-killer is covetousness. The Bible identifies covetousness as a form of idolatry. No wonder then that a covetous person is not contented. The elimination of these factors, and all other enemies of contentment, will enable the Christian to establish residence on "Serenity Street".

The positive side of the necessary devotional faith must begin with the attitude we have about the circumstances of our lives. If we are to have contentment, it is urgent that total acceptance be given to circumstances that are beyond our immediate control. Furthermore, we must learn to "accentuate the positive, and eliminate the negative," as the old song says. *We must learn to cease complaining and practice praising—in all circumstances.* We must maximize all advantages and minimize all adversities. Let me help you at this point by sharing Dot Aaron's great poem entitled "The World Is Mine":

> "Today, upon a bus, I saw a lovely maiden with golden hair;
> I envied her—she seemed so happy—and I wished I were so fair.
> *When suddenly she arose to leave,*
> *I saw her hobble down the aisle;*
> *She had one foot and wore a crutch,*
> *But as she passed, she had a smile.*
> *O God, forgive me when I whine;*
> *I have two feet—the world is mine!*
> *And when I stopped to buy some sweets,*
> *The lad who sold them had such charm.*
> *I talked with him—he said to me,*
> 'It's nice to talk with folks like you.'

'You see,' he said, 'I'm blind.'
O God, forgive me when I whine;
I have two eyes—the world is mine!
Then walking down the street,
I saw a child with eyes of blue.
He stood and watched the others play;
It seemed he knew not what to do.
I stopped for a moment, then said:
'Why don't you join the others, dear?'
He looked ahead without a word, and then
I knew he could not hear.
O God, forgive me when I whine;
I have two ears—the world is mine!
With feet to take me where I would go,
With eyes to see the sunset's glow,
With ears to hear what I would know,
O God, forgive me when I whine;
I'm blessed indeed!—The world is mine."

Most of all, Paul's motto in our text must be fully implemented in our lives: "I can do all things through Christ who keeps on infusing His strength into me." An automobile that has a functional and powerful engine beneath the hood does not need to be manually pushed down the street. A Christian who is trying by his own will-power and effort to live for Christ is disregarding the "engine" of the Christian life, the indwelling and infilling Presence and Power of Christ Himself. But a Christian who is doing all things in the strength of Christ is being used by God to demonstrate the character and conduct of Jesus to the world. Believe me, that person will be contented!

Again, we must be sure that we understand Paul's "secret of serenity" stated in verse thirteen: "I can do all things through Christ who keeps on infusing me with His strength." The secret is in the proper relation and the proper balance between "I" and "Christ." Not "I only," as if Christian living depended entirely upon me. Nor is it, "not I at all," as if the "I" is eradicated and eliminated, and Christ is the only one acting. So it is not "Christ only," as if He lives the life for me, within me, and in total disregard of me. No, it is "I through Christ." So the Christian life is not a mere circle with "I" at the center, or a circle with only "Christ" at the center. It is a two-centered ellipse ("I in you, and you in me," Jesus said), with the "I" surrendered to Christ, and Christ infusing the "I" with His strength.

You will remember that I said earlier that a Christian is to have victory in life, death, and eternity. Since sudden, violent, tragic death have been much in the news recently and would seem to be a coming threat to other Americans, let me address the subject of death in the conclusion of this study. You see, the Gospel is really true. *When a person dies in Christ, death is eternal gain.* "To me to live is Christ, and to die is gain," Paul said in Philippians 1:21. Life is but a moment when compared to eternity. The best life on earth is poor compared to eternal life in Heaven. And death (from whatever cause) is the means of transition from one life to The Other. So a Christian can even learn contentment in facing death, and each Christian should do so.

The doctor said to the young parents, "I hate to be the bearer of sad news, but your little daughter is incurably ill." After days of searching agony, the devout Christian couple said sincerely, "God's will be done." Then they debated the question, "Should we tell her? After all, she's nine years of age and has received Jesus as her Savior. She is older than her years, so why shouldn't we prepare her?"

There in the quiet of the hospital room with their only daughter the father said, "Darling, I want to talk to you about something that is very hard for me to say. The doctors say that you have a disease that they can't cure. We have prayed that God would heal you, but it seems to be His will that He take you to Heaven to live with Him. Very soon now, it will be like God sends a long train to get you and take you to the beautiful city where He lives."

Quick as a flash, the little girl's face lighted up as she looked into her daddy's eyes and said, "Daddy, will Jesus be at the station to meet me?" The father smiled tenderly as he said assuringly, "You bet he will, Darling! And what's more, Mother and Daddy will be on another train soon to join you." I repeat, a Christian who is taught in Christ's school can have contentment in life and in death, and His eternity is guaranteed! Let this thought linger beyond the reading of these words: Every Christian should have victory in life and death, and be contented in both. And His eternity is guaranteed!

Chapter 25

Behind the Seens

"But I rejoiced in the Lord greatly, that now at the last your care of me hath flourished again; wherein ye were also careful, but ye lacked opportunity. Not that I speak in respect of want: for I have learned, in whatsoever state I am, therewith to be content. I know both how to be abased, and I know how to abound: every where and in all things I am instructed both to be full and to be hungry, both to abound and to suffer need. I can do all things through Christ which strengtheneth me. Notwithstanding ye have well done, that ye did communicate with my affliction. Now ye Philippians know also, that in the beginning of the gospel, when I departed from Macedonia, no church communicated with me as concerning giving and receiving, but ye only. For even in Thessalonica ye sent once and again unto my necessity. Not because I desire a gift: but I desire fruit that may abound unto your account. But I have all, and abound: I am full, having received of Epaphroditus the things which were sent from you, an odor of a sweet smell, a sacrifice acceptable, wellpleasing to God." (Philippians 4:10-18)

I have wanted for a long time to prepare studies on the theme, "Behind the Seens." The New Testament records it as a "given," as something that should be taken for granted because it is true, that there is a *seen* world of reality, and an *unseen* world of reality. Paul summarized it in II Corinthians 4:17 when he said, "We look not at the things which are seen, but at the things which not seen: for the things which are seen are temporal; but the things which are not seen are eternal." Just seven verses later (5:7), he added, "For we walk be faith, not be sight." So there are two worlds of reality, the world of seen realities, and the world of unseen realities. If one is more real than the other, it is the world of unseen realities.

The New Testament is written by people of faith, people who live as if they are standing in both worlds. They seem always to read this world through the reality of the other world. What they are saying at any moment is based on a far bigger foundation than the immediate message and the immediate moment. The text for this study is a good example. The message of the text could be outlined in this manner: it refers to the *contribution* which the Philippian church had made to Paul and his ministry (Philippians 4:10, 14-17a), to the *contentment* Paul had found by God's grace in all the "ups and downs" of life (Philippians 4:11-12), and then to the *confidence* Paul had in the sufficiency of Christ (Philippians 4:13). So the outline appears like this:

I. The Philippians' CONTRIBUTION to Paul
II. Paul's CONTENTMENT in all situations
III. Paul's CONFIDENCE in the sufficiency of Christ

This is a grand text, but the foundation beneath these three ideas is far grander than the ideas of the local text. Behind (and beneath) the matter of a financial gift which the Philippians had sent to Paul in his need lies a deep and strong foundation of truth about financial stewardship. Behind (and beneath) the matter of Paul's contentment rests a vast foundation of revealed truth about the peace and serenity which God gives to His believing children. And behind (and beneath) the statement of Paul's confidence in the sufficiency of Christ is a whole foundation of truth about the resources we have through our identification with Christ and union with Him. Many, many people pass glibly and selfishly through life, never realizing in the slightest way what they are missing. They live only in one world, and think it is the only one. G. K.

Chesterton once said, "Most people live all their lives in the basement of life -- and think it is the living room." What surprises await them when they realize they have anchored their entire existence to an inferior world which, as wonderful as it may be, can never satisfy them as God-created human beings. *In fact, they (the secularists) think we (the Christians) are foolish!*

I want to show you in just one of the three points of the outline the connection between this local text and the larger foundational passage. Since the first part of this text (or the first part I want to deal with) has to do with a gift of money which the Philippians had sent to Paul, I am going to practice the analogy of Scripture (letting Scripture interpret Scripture) and go back to Jesus' own words about financial matters. At the end of the study from the Sermon on the Mount, I will return to this text and explain some of the financial terms that are used in it. So brace yourself for Jesus' wise and powerful words about your ("your") money.

WHERE WILL YOUR MONEY SPEND ETERNITY?

Lay not up for yourselves treasures upon earth, where moth and rust doth corrupt, and where thieves break through and steal: But lay up for yourselves treasures in heaven, where neither moth nor rust doth corrupt, and where thieves do not break through nor steal: For where your treasure is, there will your heart be also. The light of the body is the eye: if therefore thine eye be single, thy whole body shall be full of light. But if thine eye be evil, thy whole body shall be full of darkness. If therefore the light that is in thee be darkness, how great is that darkness! No man can serve two masters: for either he will hate the one, and love the other; or else he will hold to the one, and despise the other. Ye cannot serve God and mammon. (Matthew 6:19-24)

There was a long period of years at the beginning of my ministry when I would have begun a sermon on money with an apology. I have since arrived at the conviction that no preacher should ever apologize for speaking about money. A stockbroker who leads people to invest wisely in earthly enterprises does them a favor. Similarly, a preacher is a spiritual financial counselor, urging people to invest in the Lord's business and helping them to have treasure eternally.

Never once did Jesus apologize for preaching on money, and He preached about money as much as any preacher ever has. One out of every six verses that record the sayings of Jesus is on the subject of money; of the thirty-eight parables he spoke, sixteen of them, or nearly one-half, deal directly with money; *He spoke more about money than He did about heaven, hell and salvation all combined together.* In the entire Bible, for every verse on prayer, there are four verses on money. Dr. P. S. Henson was undoubtedly right when he said, "There is more religion in money than people have supposed."

The text is located at the very heart of the Sermon on the Mount. The Sermon on the Mount has been appropriately called "The Constitution of the Kingdom of Heaven." Like every good constitution, it has a financial section, the part that deals with the income and support of the Kingdom. Take a look with me at the financial section of the Constitution of the Kingdom.

A NEGATIVE WARNING

The financial section of the Kingdom Constitution opens with a *negative warning.* "Lay not up for yourselves treasures on earth." This is a universal warning — the poor man as well as the rich man may be guilty of violation. If a man spends all of his earthly possessions on himself and on earthly things, he is guilty of violating this negative command of Jesus. There are two reasons stated in this text for the negative warning given here.

First, no Christian should lay up treasures on earth and ignore God's will for his money for the simple reason that *a man's heart will follow his treasure.* In verse 21, Jesus said, "Where your treasure is, there will your heart be also." Now, this is the exact opposite of what we so often say to one another. We say, "Get a man's heart right with God, and his pocketbook will take care of itself," and this is often correct. However, it is not nearly as reliable as what Jesus said. He said, "Get a man's treasure, and you will get his heart, also." If your treasure is dedicated to God, your heart will be, also. If your treasure is not dedicated to God, then neither will your heart be.

The principle is simple: *a man's interests are where his investments are.* Would anyone say Jesus was wrong? Make no mistake about it, when our treasure is in the stock market, or in plumbing fixtures, or in homes and cars, or in vacation trips, or in pensions, there is where our heart is going to be, also. John Simpson put it this way: "A man's soul travels the same road as his money. If his money travels the high road, so will his soul; if his money travels down the low road, so will his soul." This is exactly what Jesus said. When the Bible speaks of "your treasure," it is not talking about your nickels or dimes or even a few dollars. It is talking about your total financial resources. Walter R. Fruit said, "Push your treasure out ahead of you to God, and see how your heart will follow it." Your heart follows your treasure.

Then Jesus gave another reason for this negative warning. "Lay not up treasures on earth" because *earthly treasures will enslave the heart,* He says. In verse 24, we read, "No man can serve two masters . . . . God and Mammon." "Mammon" is the Aramaic word for wealth. The word "serve" means "to be a slave to." No man can be a slave to two masters, Jesus said. No man can be under the absolute control of two different masters. And both masters named here demand total loyalty. One or the other of them will become the supreme dominating force in life. To "lay up treasures" on earth is to automatically yield to the control of Mammon, the god of wealth.

An old backwoods hunter was out to get some wild turkeys. He set a box right in their path with a trap door attached to a string. He put some corn in the box and then sat down at the edge of the clearing to manipulate the string. He watched, and in a little while, eleven wild turkeys were lured to the trap. Ten of them went into the box. One was left outside. The man waited. He thought he should have all eleven, but in a moment three of them walked out. One of the three came back in. He thought to himself, "I don't want to lose the other two," so he waited for them. Then five went out and that alarmed him, for there were only three left. If he could get two of them back in, he would let down the door. But instead two more went out and there was only one left. Well, he couldn't possibly face that at home, so he waited a while but finally the one walked out. *When all you want is to get, you finally don't want what you get.*

And for a person to attempt to divide his interest between earthly treasures and the Kingdom of God means that he forfeits the possibility of ever being under the sole control of Jesus Christ as absolute Lord of his life. You know what happens when a man tries to divide between God and Mammon; the things of God fade from the vision, the love of God declines from the heart, the soul is no longer single in its purpose, the eye becomes dim, the spiritual focus is abated, and moral and spiritual paralysis set in. So Jesus opens the financial statement of the Kingdom Constitution with a negative warning.

A POSITIVE ENCOURAGEMENT

Then, Jesus progresses a step further. He gives a *positive encouragement* to citizens of the Kingdom. "Lay up for yourselves treasures in heaven." I think it is the half-hearted hope and ambition of many people to "lay up treasures in heaven," but many of these hopes are only air-castles. How does a person go about laying up treasures in heaven?

First, you must *open an account there*. You cannot deposit money to your name in a bank if you have no account there. Proper procedure demands first arranging for an account. Similarly, to get credit for eternal treasure you must first have your name on heaven's register. You must have your name inscribed in the Lamb's book of life. The question is, Have you personally received Christ into your heart, and trusted Him totally for your eternal salvation? If you have not trusted Him to save you, you cannot make an investment in eternal treasures because you have no account in heaven. *You open the account by making a crucial deposit.* Your soul must first be deposited in Christ's keeping for eternal salvation.

The Apostle Paul stated the transaction plainly in his own personal testimony in II Timothy 1:12, where he wrote, "I know Whom I have believed, and I am persuaded that He is able to keep (guard) that which I have committed unto Him (deposited with Him) against that day."

Because this verse (II Tim. 1:12) is so crucial in understanding what I call the "salvation deposit," let me analyze the verse more carefully, identifying the parts of the salvation transaction from this verse. First, there is *a release* mentioned in Paul's testimony. "I have deposited," he said. What had he deposited into Christ's care? Himself. His total life. He had released himself into the care and use of Another, Jesus Christ. Dear friend, have you been to God's Bank of Grace and made the deposit of your whole life, of yourself, into Christ's care and use?

Second, there is *a reliance* mentioned in Paul's testimony. "I have believed," Paul said. Indeed, he said, "I know Whom I have believed." Paul had believed a Person. The word "believe" is a contracted form of two Latin words which mean, "by life." Your "belief" is what you live by; all the rest is only religious talk. If you do not live by Jesus Christ, you do not believe Him. If you do not live by the truths of the Bible, you do not believe them. The Amplified Bible defines the word "believe" by using a set of synonyms: "to trust, to cling to, to rely on." Does your life reflect a vital, living trust in the vital, living Christ? Do you cling to Him with a two-fisted grip of faith? Do you rely absolutely and totally on Him and Him alone for your eternal salvation and your daily life?

Third, there is *a relationship* pictured in Paul's testimony. Note the three personal pronouns which refer to Jesus: "Whom . . He ... Him." And note the connections between Paul and "Him" pictured: Paul believes in Him, Paul has deposited Himself into His care and us, and Paul is powerfully persuaded that He is fully able and willing to guard the deposit he has made. These words picture a deep-as-life personal relationship between Paul and Jesus Christ.

Fourth, there is *a result* pictured in Paul's testimony. "He (Jesus) is able to keep that which I have deposited with Him." The second a person trusts Jesus Christ totally and absolutely, *God mounts guard over his deposit.* This is the meaning of the word, "keep." This is the same word which is used in Luke 2 of the action of the shepherds in Bethlehem's fields on the night of Jesus' birth. Actually, the word is used twice. They were "keeping watch over their flocks by night" (King James Version). But the word is actually repeated, and it is our word, "guard." The shepherds were "guarding guard" over their sheep. It is also the same word in Acts 12 that describes the action of the four quaternions (sixteen) of soldiers who were guarding Peter in his prison cell. This word pictures the security of our salvation. Just as your bank deposits are secured by the Federal Deposits Insurance Corporation in the United States, *your salvation deposit is guaranteed by the Faith Deposits Assurance Corporation of Heaven!*

Then, you can lay up treasures in heaven by worthy, dedicated Christian giving. This is the way Jesus referred to in this passage for laying up treasure in heaven. Give your earthly wealth to the Kingdom of God and it will be transformed into heavenly treasures. There is a very interesting background behind these words. When Jesus spoke these words, the Jews were under Roman rule. The currency system was Roman. Roman money was used in commerce and society. However, the Jews refused to desecrate the temple by the use of Roman money in their giving. When they went from the marketplace, where Roman money was used, to the temple, where Jewish currency was used, they had to exchange some of their Roman money into temple currency in order to give their tithes and offerings to the temple treasury. This explains why there were always money-changers on hand in the vestibule of the temple. It was their business to exchange the street currency to temple currency, the secular coins to sacred coins. Now Jesus may be saying this: By your dedicated, worshipful investments of your money and substance to the work of the Kingdom of God, you exchange earth's currency for Heaven's; you transform earthly money into heavenly riches.

It was Pat Neff, who is a former governor of Texas, a former President of Baylor University, and a former President of the Souther Baptist Convention, who gave this testimony in his presidential address before the Southern Baptist Convention in Miami, Florida. He said, "All my life I have heard preachers tell their congregations to lay up treasures in heaven, but none has ever told me exactly how to get my treasures into heaven. I had to figure it out for myself. The only way to get our treasures into heaven is to put them into something that is going to heaven. Cattle, lands, houses, stocks and bonds, oil, coal, and the like are not going to heaven. Only men, women, boys, and girls are going to heaven. Therefore, if I am to lay up treasures in heaven, I must put them to work in the mighty task of redeeming souls that will be fit for heaven!" How true his words were! The greatest agency in the world for the redemption of men is Christ's church. Dedicated giving to His Church is a way to lay up treasures in heaven.

A PLAIN CONTRAST

Then this text offers *a plain contrast*.

First, there is a *contrast in treasures*. Every man has a treasure of some kind or another. There are only two places where a man's treasure may be located — "in heaven" or "on earth." Our choice is strictly limited to these two places. There is no third place where our treasures may be located.

What does it mean to "lay up treasures on earth?" It simply means to be supremely concerned for things. It means to so possess little "things" that you are unwilling to part with them for God's sake and for His work. Earthly treasure is a tangible, material treasure.

On the other hand, treasures in heaven cannot be seen. Now, this provides many people with the excuse they look for to refuse to give their money to the cause of Christ. Priding themselves in their practical attitude, they say, "A bird in the hand is worth two in the bush." But treasures in heaven are real treasures, though they may be unseen at this moment. And there will come a day when the man who now has earthly treasures alone will neither have one kind nor the other. In II Corinthians 4:18, the Bible says, "The things which are seen are temporal, but the things which are not seen are eternal." Treasures in heaven are now a matter of faith, but then they will be a matter of sight.

Then, there is *a contrast in investments*.

An investment in "treasures on earth" is, at best, only a temporary investment. If it draws interest which accrues even weekly, it still lasts for only a short while.

An investment in "treasures in heaven" is an eternal investment. What you invest in ministering to others is capital laid up in God's bank, the interest of which will always be accruing for you. When someone said, "George Washington threw a dollar across the Potomac," another added, "Maybe so, but a dollar went a lot further then than it does now." Dollars travel farther, last longer, and draw greater dividends when they are invested for eternity.

Then, finally, there is *a contrast in securities* pictured here.

Earthly treasures have little security. When Jesus refers to "moth, rust, and thieves," He is revealing the kind of treasures people kept in those days. They kept their wealth in garments or precious metals. Great value resided in garments. Jacob gave Joseph a coat of many colors. Joseph gave five changes of raiment to Benjamin. Achan cursed Israel because he wrongly coveted a Babylonian garment from Jericho. Samson promised thirty changes of garments to the one who guessed his riddle. Naaman brought five changes of raiment to the king of Israel. Clothing was considered to be of great value. But in one short night, moths could reduce a whole wardrobe of garments to shredded lace-work. Essentially the same thing was true of money or precious metals. There were no banks in those days; the money was hidden for security or kept in the safest place in the house. Remember Jesus' story about the treasure buried in the field. Two things might happen to it — rust might destroy it, or thieves could easily "dig through" the mud walls of the strongest house and steal the treasure. You see, there is no guaranteed security for "treasures on earth." As the writer of Ecclesiastes said, "They make themselves wings and fly away."

On the other hand, however, treasures laid up in heaven have a guaranteed security. They cannot be destroyed by moth, rust, or thieves. To put it bluntly, Jesus is simply saying this: "You can't take it with you, but you can send it on ahead of you so that it will be waiting for you when you get there, and working for you in the meantime. The treasures in heaven remain forever untarnished, utterly secure. Examining, then, your security, choose your investment accordingly.

Years ago, the secretary of a British Missionary Society called on a Calcutta merchant and asked him to help in the work. He wrote a check for $250 and handed it to the visitor. At that moment a man rushed in with a telegram in his hand. The merchant read it and then looked up with a troubled countenance. "This cablegram tells me that one of my ships has been wrecked and the cargo was lost. It makes quite a difference in my financial affairs. I'll have to write you another check." The missionary understood perfectly and handed back the check for $250. When he was handed the new check, he read it with amazement. It was written for $1,000! "Haven't you made a mistake?" the missionary asked. "No," replied the merchant, with tears in his eyes, "I haven't made a mistake. *That cablegram was a message from my Father in heaven. It said, 'Lay not up for yourselves treasures on earth.'*"

An old story is told about Dean Swift, the great scholarly preacher. He had been asked to preach a charity sermon, but he had a reputation for long-windedness, so it was tactfully suggested to him that his sermon would be most effective if it was short. So when he got up to preach, he read his text, and then spoke one sentence. The text was Proverbs 19:17, "He that hath pity on the poor lendeth unto the Lord, and that which he hath given will He pay him again." The sentence he spoke was, *"If you like the security, then put down your money."*

Now, with this foundational passage in mind, let me show you how Paul builds on these ideas in his great statement of appreciation to the Philippians for the gift they have given to him in his "affliction" (imprisonment and financial emergency, Phil. 4:14).

Paul almost playfully tells the Philippians that they have "opened an account" in heaven through their giving (verse 17). He says that their "balance sheet" ("giving and receiving," verse 15) has a large credit balance because of their generous gift. He says that their gift is like a deposit, and will draw eternal interest ("fruit," or "a dividend of interest," verse 17), and the interest rate is "abounding." Not satisfied that he has fully told everything, he uses two additional metaphors — the metaphor of a newly budding tree (the word translated "flourished" means "blossomed" in verse 10), and the metaphor of the Old Testament sacrificial system (he says that their gift had "an odor of a sweet smell, a sacrifice acceptable, well-pleasing to God"). In other words, he counsels his friends in Philippi to recognize that any gift they give to Christian work is a gift given directly to God Himself, and He finds great pleasure in such gifts! What wise financial advice, what marvelous investment wisdom, awaits the careful student of this passage. No wonder one commentator said about this passage, "There is clear gain in consulting every possible translation of the Bible on this passage."

I pray that the Holy Spirit will translate these truths to our understanding, and illumine our hearts to agreement with Himself. *Keep praying, praising, trusting, building people, and giving for the glory of God.*

Chapter 26

God's Promise of Provision

"*But my God shall supply all your need according to His riches in glory by Christ Jesus*"*(Philippians 4:19).*

The circumstances which occasioned these words were touchingly human. The Apostle Paul was imprisoned and impoverished because of his missionary ministry and message. However, he had received an encouraging love-gift from the little church at Philippi far away. His heart overflowed with appreciation, and he wrote to acknowledge their kindness and thank them for it. When he records this verse, he rises above the circumstance and expresses a God-given pledge to all Christians of the Divine sufficiency to meet any need which we may have. So this is not merely a promise to the Philippian Christians; it is a promise to you and me as well.

The study Bible of evangelist Dwight L. Moody had a notation beside this verse. It read:

"The Christian's Bank Note.
President of the Bank — 'my God'
Promise to pay — 'shall supply'
The amount — 'all your need'
The capital of the Bank – 'according to His riches in glory'
The Cashier's name — 'Christ Jesus'"

Here is God's great promise of provision to the giving Christian.

THE SOURCE OF OUR PROVISION

First, Paul identifies the *source* of our provision. "My God shall supply all your need," he says. Seven times in his letter to the Philippians, Paul uses the pronoun, "my." He writes of "my grace" (1:7), "my hope" (1:20), "my joy" (2:2 and 4:1), "my Lord" (3:8), and "my God" (1:3 and 4:19). It is an extraordinary sort of prisoner who speaks of "my grace," "my hope," and "my joy" from a prison cell! In our text, he speaks confidently, affectionately and possessively of "my God."

Now, this term may be used in a blasphemous manner. It is often used today, in public and in private (it has become a commonplace on television), as a mild exclamation and as a blasphemous oath. In fact, almost every use of it by many people is nothing but a blasphemous oath. When God said, "Thou shalt not take the name of the Lord thy God in vain," He was speaking of the very usage for which many people employ His name today. If men were wise, they would be conscientious to not use God's name in such a manner, because "He will not hold him guiltless who takes His name lightly." The Bible is surely expressing a dire reality when it says that "it is a fearful thing to fall into the hands of the living God."

But happily, this term, "my God," may also be used beautifully and believingly. Who is this God whom Paul calls "my God"? He is the God and Father of our Lord Jesus Christ, and He is our God through faith in Christ. We are His — by creation, by election, by redemption, and by donation. But it is just as wonderful to know that He is ours. Indeed, He is mine! And the One who is mine has promised to provide for me. But the promise is only made to those who can truly say, "He is my God." Is He yours through faith in Jesus Christ? "My God" is the source of my provision.

THE SURETY OF OUR PROVISION

Second, we see the *surety* of our supply in the words, "My God shall supply all your needs."

Consider the definiteness of the promise. The word "shall" is too definite for us to ever be let down. Note, too, the dimensions of our supply. The word "supply" means to "fulfill," or to "fill full." This is the same word that is used in verse 18, where Paul said, "I am full." So our need is like a giant empty vessel, and God's supply fills it to the brim. What a promise! And God watches over His Word to fulfill it, however he may choose to do so.

A dear old Christian lady lived all alone, and she lived at a very poor level of existence. On one occasion, she had spent her last penny and was just finishing her last loaf of bread. As she had often done, she got down on her knees and asked God to give her that day her daily bread (Matthew 6:11). Because it was a hot summer day, the windows of her house were open. A gang of godless ruffians were passing by. They paused at her window, and sneeringly listened to her prayer. They decided to have some unbelieving fun at the expense of this simple believing woman. They bought a loaf of bread, and when she prayed again, they dropped it on the floor just inside her window. She looked up from her prayer, saw the bread, and immediately began to profusely thank God for it. The boys then disclosed themselves, laughing cynically as they told her of their prank. "You see, God didn't hear your prayer. We brought you the bread, not God!" She smiled gently and answered, "No, laddies, ye are mistaken. It was the Lord who sent the bread — even if he used some of the devil's boys to deliver the package!" The promise is absolutely certain, no matter how God fulfills it.

THE SUFFICIENCY OF OUR PROVISION

Third, Paul points out the *sufficiency* of God's provision. "My God shall supply all your need," he wrote. Give special attention to the inclusive word, "all." It is not some of your need, or much of your need, or merely most of your need that God will supply, but all of your need. So this is a great promise of abundant provision.

The presence of need in our lives is obvious, isn't it? Each of us is full of needs. We have needs of body, needs of mind, needs of heart, and needs of spirit. Our human nature is one great bundle of needs, always crying aloud for satisfaction. When considering such a promise, it is necessary to distinguish carefully between our needs and our greeds, between our necessities and our desires. On one occasion, Paul prayed for a certain "thorn in the flesh" to be removed from his life (II Cor. 12:1-10). But, though Paul requested removal, he actually received reinforcement. Paul understood his need to be removal of the grievance, but God understood his need to be the reinforcement of grace. An old television program was named, "Father Knows Best", but that is not always true of any human father. However, it is perfectly true of our Heavenly Father, and He always meets our needs according to His understanding of them.

Though the presence of need is obvious, the purpose of need is often obscure. Need is your dearest friend — if it brings you to God. You see, God gives us needs that He might give us Himself.

The provision of our needs is overwhelming. "All our needs" will be met! Our needs are as varying as our personalities, as different as our circumstances, as distinctive as our temptations — but they will be met! There is a very interesting Greek word that is used twice in Peter's first letter, and it is surely no coincidence that the word is used in two texts which reveal a matching resource for each of our needs. It is translated "manifold" in our Bibles. In I Peter 1:6, the Holy Spirit refers to "manifold temptations," testings, or trials. Then in I Peter 4:10, He refers to "manifold grace." The word actually means "many-colored," referring both to the different human conditions it meets, and to the different contributions that God makes to meet those conditions.

This exercise will help us to understand the meaning. Let your left hand represent these trials, testings, and temptations — all the needs of your life. The thumb and each finger are all distinct and different, standing for your different needs. Then let your right hand represent the Divine resources which match each of those needs. Note that the digits on each hand coincide and correspond to those on the other. So God's resources correspond to, and cover, our requirements. Surely God's supply is given to meet our needs, but it is probably truer to say that our needs are Divinely given to arouse our dependence upon God for His supply.

THE STANDARD OF OUR PROVISION

Fourth, our verse points out the *standard* of God's provision. "My God shall supply all our needs according to His riches in glory," Paul said. Practically, this means that it is not possible for us to have a need that is too great for God to supply.

A cursory reading of Paul's letters will reveal how fond he was of the word "riches." In Romans 2:4, he spoke of "the riches of God's goodness." In Roman 11:33, he wrote of "the riches of His wisdom." In Ephesians 1:7, he mentioned "the riches of His grace." Ephesians 1:18 refers to "the riches of His glory." When the prodigal son had descended to the depths "in the far country" in degradation and deprivation, his redemption began when he remembered that there was "enough and to spare" in his father's house. The word "enough" reveals how much is laid up for us in our Father's house, and the additional words, "and to spare," point out how God delights to give — up to the limit of our need, and a bit more! Paul wrote that God is "rich in mercy" in Ephesians 2:4. When we finally begin to get a tiny hint in our hearts of the vast meaning of Paul's words and the even more vast treasury of God's wealth, we tend to echo the words of the Queen of Sheba who came to Jerusalem to see the renowned wealth of King Solomon for herself. After she had witnessed his vast wealth with her own eyes, she sighed, "The half was not told me." Pastor Erwin Lutzer wrote a fine little book on the believer's wealth in Christ, entitled, *Christian, You Are Richer Than You Think!*

It has occasionally been noted that God does not merely give to His children out of His riches, or from His riches, but rather according to His riches. If I appealed to a very wealthy man for financial assistance and he gave me $100, he would have given me a gift out of His riches, or from his riches, but the gift would certainly not be according to His riches. All the gifts provided for us by God's grace are lavish and abundant, "according to His riches in glory."

THE STOREHOUSE OF OUR PROVISION

Fifth, the text reveals the *storehouse* in which our provision is kept, and from which it comes. "My God shall supply all your need according to His riches in glory by Christ Jesus." All of God's provisions of grace are "packaged up" for us in Christ, and they come to us through Christ. The source is in Christ Jesus, and the supply is by Christ Jesus. One commentator wrote, "Here is a bank that never breaks; no demand made upon it will find it wanting, or unready — for 'it' is He." Everything, literally everything, God has for us is in Christ Jesus. Come, then, you sinners and you saints: here is God's Plenty; here is grace truly abounding.

Horace Hull was at one time one of the owners and operators of the Hull-Dobbs Ford dealership in Memphis, and was a leading layman in a large Methodist church there. One weekend, he, his wife and a housemaid had gone on a visitation trip to northeast Georgia to visit family members. When they started home again, they had not gone far when they ran into a blinding rainstorm. Mr. Hull slowed his car to a "snail's pace" and was driving slowly down the highway when a huddled group of people suddenly loomed before them on the edge of the highway. He eased his car around them and stopped. It proved to be a family of wife, husband, and several children, huddled under a bed sheet as they walked down the highway. When Mr. Hull enquired, he discovered that their house has just burned a short time before, and they were trying to reach a neighbor's house to "regroup." Mr. Hull opened his car doors, and the three of them made room for the entire family in the car. They began to move forward again, and he turned off the road to a nearby farmhouse at the father's instructions. When they pulled up in front of the house, Mr. Hull pulled out his wallet and removed a five dollar bill. "Here," he said to the mother and wife, "maybe this will help." The mother wore a forlorn and mournful look, but she took the money with a mumbled word of thanks. The family got out of the car, mounted the steps to the porch, and Mr. Hull and his wife and maid pulled out toward the highway again.

Mr. Hull said he had only gone a few feet when the Holy Spirit of God spoke to him, convicting him of his meager contribution to match a great need. He stopped the car and said to his wife and the maid, "Open your purses and empty out all the cash you have." They did so, and he matched their action. He then added a sizeable check to the cash amount, and they turned the car around and drove back to the house. They honked the horn of the car until the family emerged again from the farmhouse. Mr. Hull beckoned for the man and wife to get back into his car, which they did. When they were seated in the rear seat, he asked, "Ma'am, how much did I give you awhile ago?" "Five dollars," she replied. "Give it back!" he exclaimed, steadily looking into her eyes. Her look demonstrated dismay over his apparent hardness and coldness. "Give it back!" he commanded again. She opened her hand and returned the crumpled five dollar bill. Then he took his hat, into which he had placed the cash and the check which he had collected, lifted it over the back of the front seat — and dumped all the money into her lap. He explained the reason for his action, prayed with the family, wished them well, and then departed again, far more satisfied about his involvement in their sad situation.

Again, Horace Hull said that he had only driven a short distance down the highway when the Holy Spirit of God spoke plainly to him. "My son," He said, "did you get the lesson?" While Mr. Hull pondered the question, the Holy Spirit said, "I have given you one life — even if it is only about a five dollar life! Then one day, I came to you and said, 'Give it back.' You hesitated and argued, 'But I only have one life.' I insisted, 'Give it back!' You finally saw that I can do a great deal more with your life than you can, and you gave it back. And from that day to this, I have opened the windows of heaven upon your life, and dumped all of My riches into your lap!" What an illustration of our text!

One Mother's Day, two little girls gave to their mother a homemade book which they called, "Our Promise Book." On each page, there was a childish drawing, accompanied by a promise, such as, "I promise to wash the dishes after each meal for one day." The book contained instructions for the mother: when she tore out any particular page and presented it to one of the girls, she was "cashing in" the promise for that day. There was a page for each day in a month. The mother was delighted over this present, and discovered that the girls' promises could be trusted. Friends, the Bible is God's Promise Book to us. The number of promises in it are astronomical, and they await our faith to "cash them in."

Pastor Thomas De Witt Talmage told years ago of a man who returned from New York to London after suffering business failure in the United States. He threw himself down in a chair in his London home and said mournfully, "Everything is gone." His wife asked, "What do you mean?" He replied, "I have had to suspend payment on our home; nothing is left." His little boy sensed the father's sadness, and bounding into his lap, he said, "Father, you have me left." And the wife, who had been very sympathetic and helpful throughout his financial ordeal, said, "And, my dear, you have me left." And the old grandmother, seated in a corner of the room, pushed her spectacles up on her nose as she said, "But most of all, son, you have all the promises of God left."

Each promise of God is as solid as a sack of cement. But everyone knows that cement must be mixed with water. To be fully effective, each promise of God must be mixed with faith. I (and every other believer) should make it my testimony and my trust daily that, as I walk with Him on His terms, "my God shall supply all of my needs according to His riches in glory by Christ Jesus." Hallelujah!

Wolfgang Mozart, the great Austrian musician, was walking one day in the suburbs of Vienna when he was met by a beggar. The beggar told a tale of personal misfortune with such effect that it aroused the interest of the great composer in his favor. But the supply in Mozart's purse at the moment did not match the impulse of his compassion. So he asked the beggar to follow him to a local coffee house. Here Mozart drew a folded sheet of paper from his pocket and composed a musical score on it. He then wrote a letter and gave both the composition and the letter to the beggar, telling him to take them to his publisher. A composition from Mozart was a "check payable at sight" with his publisher at any time. The letter explained that the publisher was to give the amount to the beggar who brought the composition to him. The happy beggar was immediately given a good sum of money when he presented the musical manuscript to the publisher.

Friends in faith, what an advantage it is to have a Divine Friend Who has unlimited credit in Heaven and in Whose Name we may come at any time to the treasure house when we are in need! No check on the bank of Heaven, presented in the name of God's own Dear Son, can be rejected for lack of funds. His merits and His resources are available to us, which means the covering of every need, not only for the brief years of time, but for all eternity.

A reading of Philippians 4:11-15 will reveal that Paul was using an illustration from commercial life, or from the world of finance, when he wrote the background to our text. If you are without Christ, I encourage you to give special attention to his first two ideas. If you are a Christian, I encourage you to give special attention to his last two ideas. Here are the key ideas:

(1) It is the course of eternal wisdom to form a partnership with Heaven's God and His people. This partnership is established the moment a person is saved. If you have not been saved, confess your sins directly to God at this moment, and repent of them. Realize that God has loved you in spite of your sins and unworthiness, and that He lovingly sent His Son to the earth to die for you and your sins. Remember that Jesus rose again from the dead, and

that all of this was for you. He said that if you would trust Him as your own risen Savior, He would save you the very moment you totally trust Him. Do so at this moment. Then recognize that you have entered a lifetime partnership with the Lord of the universe, and let Him govern your life.

(2) You must open an account for the practice of "giving and receiving," suggested in verse 15. Your entire life is to be an inhale-exhale type of exercise, alternating regularly between receiving and giving.

If a country is going to be economically viable and healthy, its export trade must properly balance its import trade. One reason for the extraordinary prosperity of the United States has been its historic ability to balance its exports and imports, even exceeding its imports by its exports. When this rule fails, there is economic trouble in the land. In the Christian life, also, if we are to prosper spiritually we must "export" in giving and in service to others in proportion to the amount we have received in blessing. Many are stalemated in their Christian lives simply because they do not give out to others in a measure proportionate to God's blessings to them. Jesus said, "Freely ye have received, freely give" (Matthew 10:8). This is the practice of giving and receiving Paul refers to in these verses.

(3) You should keep a record, for the sake of reminder, like a debit and credit page, of your giving and receiving. Paul apparently kept at least a mental record of the giving and receiving that was exchanged between him and the Philippian believers (verse 15).

(4) You must learn to expect dividends, or regular interest, on your investments. Read the context, and note verse 17: "Not that I seek your gift for myself, but I seek for the profit which increases to your account." Any giver knows that giving often does far more for the giver than it does for the one who receives the gift. A disciple who teaches another Christian how to give freely, bountifully, and in faith, is a good investment counselor, and he should never feel apologetic for the great service he renders!

But there is far more here than that simple principle. Every time you give to God's people or God's cause, as unto the Lord, Paul declared, the gift will draw eternal interest. Give special attention to the idea that all stewardship gifts are to be regarded as deposits in an eternal account, and that regular interest may be expected. The Christian giving of money is a sound business investment in eternal values, where dividends will accrue at compound interest for all eternity! And the same thing is certainly true of the investment of life, influence, vision, strategy, etc. (all the dimensions of disciple-making) into the lives of other believers, as well. This idea is developed extensively in Paul's letters to his disciple, Timothy.

If you are without Christ, open an account in the secure Bank of Heaven by trusting Jesus Christ today, and make your first deposit, the deposit of your life into His hands for eternal salvation. Paul was referring to this when he said, "I know Whom I have believed, and am persuaded that He is able to keep (guard) that which I have committed (deposited) unto Him against That (any) Day" (II Timothy 1:12).

Exercise firm faith in Jesus Christ today, and you will join Heaven's Faith Firm, backed by God's Faith Deposits Insurance Commitment (FDIC!), and you can begin immediately to make daily investments in The Account. And remember that you make your best investments in your eternal account in Heaven when you deposit your spiritual resources in the lives of other people here on earth — with the goal of multiplying the original investment by the deposit . You should seek to daily expand the number of beneficiaries. You will be eternally glad you did!

Chapter 27

Saints under Satan's Nose

"All the saints salute you, chiefly they that are of Caesar's household" (Philippians 4:22).

In the first chapter of his letter to the Philippians, Paul had said, "My bonds in Christ are manifest in all the palace" (Philippians 1:13). The "bonds" he referred to were the small chains he wore as he waited in Rome, attached by the chains to a Roman soldier. The word "manifest" means that his imprisonment as a Christian was widely publicized among the Roman guards, in the larger community surrounding the Roman Caesar Nero, and in the entire environment of the city of Rome. So God was using an evil circumstance in the life of Paul to publicize him and the Gospel he preached. The word "palace" is actually the Greek word praetorium. The praetorium was the large living quarters of the large Roman guard that remained in Rome to protect the throne of Caesar. The word was used for both the place and the military people who lived there. The Apostle Paul reports that his very imprisonment, which he had at first thought to be most detrimental to his ministry as an apostle and an evangelist, had instead "turned out rather for the advance of the Gospel."

In fact, the Gospel had "advanced" so widely due to this circumstance that it had penetrated "Caesar's household." We shall see in this study that that is equivalent to saying that the Gospel was spreading its fragrance "right under Satan's nose." Satan? Yes, we shall see that the Gospel was perfuming the air with the grace of God "right under Satan's nose." Our text is small, so we can easily look at the main features of Paul's statement.

A SCRIPTURAL IDENTIFICATION

First, we must be careful to make a *scriptural identification* of the persons who are highlighted by this text. "All the saints salute you," Paul said. There is a great deal of confusion surrounding the word "saint" today. Reinhold Niebuhr once remarked that a saint is the wife of a man who thinks he is one! Niebuhr's comment was only playful humor, but the abuse of the word "saint" in a great portion of the world of "Christendom" is far from humorous! Elevating whimsical tradition above the clear teaching of Scripture, one vast religious system has prevented millions of people from seeing the true Biblical meaning of the word "saint."

Many years ago, there lived in Edinburgh, Scotland, a grocer named James Saint. A man wrote a letter to him, but mistakenly addressed it to "James Saint, Aberdeen, Scotland." The postal service in Aberdeen searched for James Saint there, but could not find him. They returned the letter to its sender with this notation, "There are no Saints in Aberdeen. Try Edinburgh." This might be called "the case of the missing saint." Today's misunderstanding of the word "saint" might be equally laughable except that the destinies and eternal destination of millions of people may be at stake because of the confusion.

One Roman Catholic writer defined a saint as "a saved soul who has been made famous by exceptional virtue." Another said, "A saint, in the strict sense of the word, is one who is in the enjoyment of the beatific vision (a direct vision of God), and has been presented by the Church for public worship of the faithful." The Roman Catholic "saint" is recognized and officially designated by the Catholic Church as a saint. This official church recognition or designation of these "saints" is called "canonization." The Roman Catholic process of canonizing a saint is a long and costly one. A saint is canonized only after a careful investigation which calls for certain qualifications to have been met, including the working of miracles. As the above quotation indicates, those who are thus canonized by the Catholic Church may be worshiped, and their "works of super-erogation" (works which supposedly produce a surplus of personal merit) may then be credited to the common person who prays to them. Catholics pray to the saints, not on the ground that the saints can answer their prayer, but on the ground that they can intercede with God for the one praying. Roman Catholicism especially emphasizes that Christ will not deny anything to his Mother. It is sadly interesting at the present time to watch the Catholic Church stampeding toward an elevation of Mary to co-equality and co-essentiality with Jesus. But for millions of "believers," it will prove to be eternally tragic!

The Catholic worship of saints and relics of the saints (and similar practices) is pure superstition and idolatry. When Roman Catholics worshipfully call Mary the "Queen of Heaven" and the "Mother of God," this practice is wickedly idolatrous. Furthermore, any appeal to these "special saints" to intercede for us is an implicit denial of the sufficiency of the mediatorial work of Christ. "There is one Mediator between God and man, Himself the Man, Christ Jesus" (I Timothy 2:5). When I have that One, one is enough! His work of Atonement and Intercession is perfect and all-sufficient! To add anything to it is to terribly depreciate Jesus, and to default into the usual religious error of depending on human works for salvation.

Now to the New Testament teaching concerning "saints." In the New Testament, believers in Christ are called "saints" 56 times — even when they are carnal and sinful. In the New Testament, the word is never used in the singular; it is always plural, "saints." It is not used to refer to an individual, but to individuals as part of a fellowship of saints. So the individual isolation of some particular person to recognize his special piety is not supported by the New Testament use of the word "saints."

Furthermore, the obvious meaning of the word in the New Testament does not support the Roman Catholic view. The word "saints" translates the Greek word, *hagioi*, which is the root form for the word "holy." The emphasis of the word is on holiness, to be sure — but it is always on God's holiness, not the holiness of any man or group of men. Paul's greetings to the Corinthians (the carnal Corinthians!) will reveal this. "To the church of God which is at Corinth, to those sanctified in Christ Jesus, called to be saints together with all those who in every place call on the name of our Lord Jesus Christ, both their Lord and ours" (I Corinthians 1:2). The word "saint" means "separated, called out, set apart." The New Testament meaning is that a saint is a sinful human being who is chosen by God, called out by God, and consecrated to God and His service. And these terms are used of all believers in Christ, not a mere select few! To be a saint is not to build your own personal holiness (which no human being can do), but rather to come under the coverage of, and within the realm of, God's holiness (which every sinful human being must do, if he is to be saved). A saint is holy, not because of his own purity, but solely because he has been made holy or declared right and righteous by God on the basis of the saving work of Jesus Christ. James Earl Massey said, "A saint is a God-claimed person whose life shows that claim." Every Christian is a saint. He may be struggling with carnality while trying to face and honor the claims of Christ upon his life, but if he is truly saved, he is a saint.

Think again of I Corinthians 1:2. " . . . to those sanctified in Christ Jesus, called to be saints." The first of these two phrases is the key to the meaning of the word. We are saints because of what has been done for us — "sanctified by Christ Jesus." To be "sanctified" means to be set apart to a holiness produced by Christ and not produced through our own effort. The term is all the more surprising, even startling, even shocking, when we remember who are the recipients of this Corinthian letter. The Corinthians would be the very last congregation in the New Testament whom we would call "saints" if the word "saints" refers to keeping one's ways pure.

Every single chapter in I Corinthians deals with some specific problem of carnality that had developed in the church at Corinth (even the "love chapter," I Corinthians 13!). The Corinthian "saints" were marked by

(1) a very divisive party spirit, the problem of disunity (chapters 1-4);

(2) a serious case in incest in the church, to which the entire Body was being indifferent, the problem of immorality (chapter 5);

(3) the filing of personal lawsuits against one another over matters which should easily have been settled in the local Body; the problem of legality (chapter 6);

(4) squabbles over the single and the married state, the problem of matrimony (chapter 7);

(5) the selfish indulgence of questionable morals, thus violating weaker believers, the problem of Christian liberty (chapter 8-10);

(6) the abuse of the Lord's Supper and public worship, the problem of liturgy (chapter 11);

(7) the flagrant abuse of certain spiritual gifts for selfish purposes, the problem of spirituality (chapters 12-14);

(8) much misunderstanding of the doctrine of the bodily resurrection of Christ and the future bodily resurrection of all believers, the problem of immortality (chapter 15); and by

(9) abuses of financial stewardship, the problem of liberality (chapter 16).

And these matters were general and widespread in the entire church, so that Paul said, "You are still carnal" (I Corinthians 3:3). And yet, these very people are (each and all) referred to as "saints"!

It is evident that many saints are not very saintly at certain times of their lives. Then why are they called saints? The answer is crucial to an understanding of New Testament Christianity. They are called saints in the New Testament because God views them from the standpoint of the completed work of Christ on their behalf — and not from the present level of their spiritual growth or personal holiness! God accepted them perfectly at the moment of their trust in Christ and in His completed work on their behalf. And we should surely thank God that He receives sinners on that basis, because not one (not one — Romans 3:10) of us would have the slightest chance of an eternity with God if the Gospel of His grace and His salvation did not totally cover us. But the Good News is that it does — it does — totally — cover — even sinners like us (like me)! Hallelujah!

So the word "saint" is simply the new name of all redeemed people. The old name was "sinners" (those identified before God only by sin). The new name is "saints" (those identified before God only by salvation). The one difference between a saint and a sinner is the Saviour. The Saviour and all of His benefits are absent from the life of a sinner; the Saviour and all of His benefits are present in the life of a saint. The Philippian saints who read this letter from Paul would be reminded of some clear examples in Philippi. The first convert to Christ in Philippi (indeed, in Europe) was Lydia, who was a decent and moral sinner one moment, but a saint the next (Acts 16:13-15). The slave girl who was converted to Christ on the city streets in Philippi was a tormented sinner one moment, a saint the next (Acts 16:16-18). The Philippian jailer who was dramatically saved in an earthquake-shattered prison in Philippi was at one moment a sinner on the verge of suicide and the next a saint on his way to Heaven (Acts 16:19-34)! What made the difference? In each case, the Jesus who was outside of them came into them and instantaneously made each one of them a saint!

Paul demonstrated the all-inclusive scope of sainthood by calling all the Corinthians believers "saints together with all those who everywhere call on the name of our Lord Jesus Christ" (I Corinthians 1:2). Anybody who narrows sainthood to a restrictive group who supposedly excel in godliness (supposedly, I say), has gone far afield from New Testament teaching. If you read the epistles of the New Testament, you will discover that their total content is addressed to all the saints, that is, to all Christians, and a substantial portion of each epistle deals with the sins and struggles of these saints.

One of the great preachers and Bible teachers in America during the early twentieth century was the Chicago pastor, Dr. H. A. Ironside. During his early ministry, he was traveling by train to the Pacific Coast for a series of Bible conferences. In his railway car was a party of Catholic nuns, and each day of the long trip by train he spoke to them and they spoke to him. He would sit reading his Bible, and at times the group of nuns talked with him about spiritual things. After several conversations, he asked them if any one of them had ever seen a saint. They all quickly answered in the negative. Then he asked them if they would like to see a saint. Their faces brightened as they all agreed that they would very much like to see a saint. Then he astonished them by saying, "Then let me introduce you to a saint. I am a saint. I am saint Harry." He then opened his New Testament and showed them its clear teaching about the "saints." Harry Ironside was simply echoing the teaching of the New Testament. By the authority of the Word of God, I or any other true believer in Jesus Christ, have as much right to the title of "saint" as did Paul, Peter, or any of the apostles. And I must add that we have more right to the claim than many of those who have been "canonized" into "sainthood" while depending on their own works (actually, they have no right to claim the word for themselves at all).

So the "saints" mentioned in our text are simply everyday, garden-variety, common Christians who have been truly born again, who love Jesus, who struggle with their own flesh and their own sins, who may at any moment be in a failing condition, but who have been set apart by God unto Himself and everything that Life With Him means.

A STRANGE LOCATION

Second, we note the *strange location* of these saints. They are identified as "the saints . . . of Caesar's household." That is about the last place in the world where anyone would have expected to find Christians.

These saints are identified by their association with a certain person. The "Caesar" in the text was the Roman Emperor Nero, the last and the worst of the Roman emperors. Nero had exhausted the catalogue of crime. He poisoned his stepbrother Britannicus. He divorced, banished and then slew his wife Octavia. He kicked to death the slave paramour who had become his empress. "He bathed his body in unguents and his soul in lust," wrote one historian. Rome was accustomed to hearing of immorality and crime, but the excesses and vices of Nero astonished even Rome.

One secular historian said, "Nero far surpassed other Roman Emperors in infamy. He concentrated enough inhumanity and pollution in his person to have darkened a widespread atmosphere around himself. He expended more ingenuity in contriving new modes of dishonoring humanity than most Christians have in serving it." His murder of his own mother, wife, and son was motivated by the desire to protect his place on the imperial throne. He was the renowned arch-persecutor of Christians. He burned the city of Rome, and tried to throw the suspicion of his deed onto Christians. He tortured his Christian subjects by unheard-of torments, sewing them up in animal skins and casting them out to be devoured by dogs and wild beasts. He even had some Christians crucified. Others were smeared with pitch, impaled upon sharp spikes in the imperial gardens, and set on fire to illumine the gardens. Is it not obvious that Nero was the arch-enemy of Christians? This was the "Caesar" Paul was referring to in our text. The "saints" in the text are identified by their association with the sadistic Roman Emperor Nero.

These saints are also identified by their association with a certain place. "The saints of Caesar's household salute you." This term does not mean that they were the Caesar's family members, but rather that they were slaves and servants in his household community.

Nero's household — what an unlikely place to find Christians! Not only were the lives of these Christians in constant danger, but there was enough pagan revelry and sensual carnival in the palace area to choke the faith of any newborn believer and to threaten that of even the most mature Christian. These Christians had everything to gain by being 100 per cent Romans and Caesarites, and everything to lose by being Christians. Yet they are Christians even in this most forbidding atmosphere. They put principle above policy. They put love for God above love for life. They put Christ above Caesar.

Out of this strange combination of place and people comes a gigantic principle: Christian character and conduct may be independent of location and circumstance, however evil they may be. After all, Joseph kept his life pure even in the pagan and impure atmosphere of Egypt. Daniel maintained his prayer life and purity of conduct while serving in the pagan courts of four Babylonian rulers. Obadiah kept his conscience even in the house of Ahab. Nehemiah maintained his convictions and character even in the Persian palace. Character may be independent of atmosphere!

Just today, I reread the parable of the good and bad figs recorded in the brief twenty-fourth chapter of Jeremiah. "One basket had very good figs, even like the figs that are first ripe: and the other basket had very bad figs, which could not be eaten, they were so bad" (verse 2). The remainder of the chapter is used to explain this picture. The good figs represented the Jews who had been taken captive to Babylon, while the spoiled figs represented the Jews who had remained in their homeland. Babylon was the evil place, while Judah was the good place. But strangely, the rotten figs were in the "good" place, while the good figs were in the "rotten" place! So we have the same picture in the parable that we see in our text. Babylon with all of its environmental evils could not corrupt the captive Jews who were taken there. The actual grace on the inside of them was greater than the atmospheric guilt on the outside! Their souls were pure though their surroundings were perverted. But the situation was exactly the reverse with the Judean Jews, the Jews who remained in their homeland; their hearts were perverted while living in an environment that should have promoted purity. You see, the battle for purity is won or lost within ourselves. Jesus said, "The prince of this world cometh, and hath nothing in me" (John 14:30). Satan brought the spark of temptation to Jesus, but there was nothing in His character which could be ignited by it. Babylon may leave me unstained if my walk with God insulates me against its contamination, and Judea can become my deepest hell if my heart is impure. Saints can have victory even in Caesar's household if they will steadily abide in Christ.

There were saints in Caesar's household — and there were sinners in the Garden of Paradise! Satan and the angels which followed him fell from the perfect atmosphere of Heaven! But Jesus withstood the full onslaughts of Satan and temptation in a desolate wilderness!

While acknowledging the corruption of the atmosphere of the city of Sardis, Jesus said to the saints there, "Thou hast a few names even in Sardis which have not defiled their garments; and they shall walk with me in white: for they are worthy" (Revelation 3:4). You may be forced to live in some atmosphere worse than that of Caesar's household, worse than wicked and licentious Sardis, but you can still be "blameless and harmless, the sons of God, without rebuke, in the midst of a crooked and perverse nation, among whom you shine as lights in the world, holding forth the Word of life" (Philippians 2:15).

Sadly, many Christians today are like chameleons. Chameleons, as you know, change their color to match their environment. This is a defense mechanism (as it is with Christians, as well) for self-protection, but self-protection is not a Christian discipline. A little boy was playing with a chameleon one day. He put it on a brown rock, and it matched the color of the rock. Then he put it on a leaf, and it turned green. He repeated these actions several times, and each time there was the same result. Then he boldly put the chameleon on a friend's plaid shirt — and the chameleon had a nervous breakdown! There are far too many chameleon Christians today. They can't be transformed to the likeness of Christ because they have allowed themselves to be conformed to the world around them.

Paul seems almost to have saved the best until last when he conveyed greetings to the Philippian Christians, "especially they that are of Caesar's household." One commentator says that the word translated "especially" means "most of all" or "above all." All that Nero was, all that Nero did, and all that Nero stood for, failed to discourage these saints from standing for Christ. They were "in the world, but not of it," as Jesus had prayed that His followers would be. Caesar's household may have been the realm of their living, but it did not supply the roots and resources of their lives. "Greater is He that is in you than he that is in the world" — and these saints were proving it.

May I address a personal question to you, dear saint of God? Are you changing your surroundings, or are your surroundings changing you? Are you a spiritual thermostat or a spiritual thermometer? Do you merely register the moral climate around you, or do you regulate it by your firm, loving stand for Christ? God will so fortify a Spirit-filled saint from within, that he will not only withstand the evil pressure from without, but he will even establish beachheads for Gospel advance where he is. Our "interior climate" of trust and devotion should not be influenced by the "exterior climate" of trial and destitution. A beautiful lily may grow and bloom right out of a dismal swamp. "The best place for light is darkness." A candle is wasted in bright sunshine, but it may illuminate an entire room if the room is dark.

The great Scottish preacher, John Henry Jowett, commented on this truth with his usual penetrating insight when he said, "God's Book says that 'He maketh grass to grow upon the mountains' (Psalm 147:8). What a wonder, that the tender thing is growing on the cold and inhospitable heights! If we had found it in the sheltered valley where the dews are heavy and drenching, and where the harsh wind is softened to a wooing caress, it would have awakened little or no interest. But to find it growing 'upon the mountains,' on the very playground of the storm, in the very teeth of contending blasts — that is the marvel which fascinates us. Even so, God seems to delight in rearing His spiritual beauties in the most difficult and unlikely places, yea, in the very midst of blasphemy and desolation. He has a peculiar joy in exhibiting His saints in Caesar's household. It seems as though God's plants can laugh at circumstances, that they can sink strange roots right through their immediate setting, and reach such marvelous resources that their inhospitable environment counts for nothing. So let us address ourselves to mountain-work or wilderness-work with a courageous and singing spirit. Let us put our best into the worse. If it is mountain- work, He will use us to grow His grass there. If it is wilderness-work, He will produce 'springs in the desert' through our efforts."

A SIMPLE EXPLANATION AND A STRONG EXHORTATION

Finally, let me close this study with a *simple explanation* and a *strong exhortation*. The simple explanation is that human beings do their main living within, and it is the glory of the Christian Gospel that it offers all the necessary resources for victorious inner living. The old Puritans called it "living inly," a strange expression which reveals that they had caught the secret. A Christian will never have the outward vocation of influence and power which he should have, unless he has an inward victory of daily devotion and discipline that governs all that he is and does. If those "saints in Caesar's household" were to survive and serve, they would have to practice vital fellowship corporately with each other and vital fellowship personally with God. Paul puts them on display in his closing greeting, which means that they were doing both.

The strong exhortation: Dear Christian, give far more attention to what is happening in you than to what is happening to you.

If you live rooted deeply in Christ by faith, if you live from your elevated position in Christ in the heavenlies, you will carry your own climate of peace and power though severe storms may be raging around you. Then, as George Fox said, you will probably "light up the countryside for miles around."

Some years ago, after I had seen a National Geographic television special, a friend and I researched "the European water spider." The small creature unwittingly gave to the two of us a great illustration on the Christian life. The European water spider has a tail that is disproportionately large in comparison to the rest of its body. It uses its tail like a beaver does. It swims on the surface of the water, raises its tail, and slaps it down on the surface of the water. When it does so, a thin web-like sac gathers air and expands on its back. It looks like a thin balloon inflated and attached to the spider's back. Then the spider descends beneath the water, disconnects the sac from its body, and re-attaches it to some stationary object below the water. Then it moves into the air bubble inside the sac, and lives there until the air supply is depleted. When it needs more air, it carries the sac back to the surface and repeats the procedure again.

What a picture of a Christian! Though he lives in a threatening atmosphere, he can carry the resources from his heavenly position with him. Thus, he can happily survive and serve in the world that needs him most. Like John on the Isle of Patmos, he may be surrounded by a hostile environment and hopeless people, but if he will live "in the Spirit" as John did (Revelation 1:10), the world will be blessed by his visions and his victory until the end of time. Christian, stay faithful even if you live right under Satan's nose! It will gain the attention of those without God, the appreciation of the people of God, and God Himself will make note of it in His Record Book!